The *Active Reader*

Book 5

Linda Kita-Bradley

Grass Roots Press

Edmonton, Alberta, Canada

2011

The Active Reader – Book 5 © 2011 Grass Roots Press

The Active Reader – Book 5 is published by

Grass Roots Press
A division of Literacy Services of Canada Ltd.
www.grassrootsbooks.net

AUTHOR	Linda Kita-Bradley
PASSAGES	Contributing Writers: Rose Boll, Terry Barber
EDITOR	Pat Campbell
DESIGN	Lara Minja
LAYOUT	Susan Hunter
PILOTERS	Avril Lewis, Dyanne Manuel, Linda Stewart, Barb Pottier, Keith Finn, Julie Briand, with a special thanks to Halifax Community Learning Network

ACKNOWLEDGEMENTS

We acknowledge the financial support of the Government of Canada through the Book Publishing Industry Development Program (BPIDP) for our publishing activities.

We acknowledge the support of the Alberta Foundation for the Arts for our publishing programs.

ISBN 978-1-926583-19-8

Printed in Canada

Contents

About this workbook

Welcome to Book 5 of *The Active Reader* series. This workbook aims to engage learners in the process of active reading by (1) providing stimulating reading passages, thought-provoking discussion questions, and practical literacy activities, and (2) helping learners develop the skills and strategies to become independent readers.

The workbook is organized around five themes: people, relationships, health, the environment, and history. Each theme consists of two units that provide the following activities:

Pre-reading
Photos, cartoons, and discussion questions introduce learners to the unit topic, activate learners' background knowledge, personalize the unit topic, and provide a purpose for reading.

Main Reading Passage
Learners are encouraged to read actively through making inferences, visualizing, predicting, and making personal connections with the text. Sidebars explain vocabulary or provide additional information to enhance readers' understanding.

Post-reading
Learners discuss questions that provide further practice in making inferences and personal connections with the text as well as summarizing ideas and supporting main ideas with details. Learners are also encouraged to think beyond the text through relating key ideas and themes from the passage to current trends and events.

Summary
Learners are introduced to the concept of summarizing by rereading one or two selected paragraphs from the unit passage and choosing the best summary of the paragraph(s) from three given options.

Vocabulary
Learners deepen their understanding of target vocabulary by producing the vocabulary in discussion and writing.

Mini-Lesson
Learners focus on making inferences, finding main ideas, drawing conclusions, summarizing, and recognizing text structures.

Literacy Practice
Learners are encouraged to engage in daily literacy practices through reading, analyzing, and discussing print and visual forms such as graphs, medicine labels, political cartoons, newspaper articles, photos, and maps.

Dictionary Use
Learners determine whether statements are true or false by referring to sample dictionary entries that provide meanings for unfamiliar words or word usage. An appendix showing the parts and functions of a dictionary entry provides further support to the learner.

© CBS/Landov

People
Jane Goodall

Vocabulary: inquisitive   domestic   advocate

Mini-Lesson: Making Inferences

Literacy Practice: Website Home Page

▶▶ Discussion

"Animals have rights, too."
Do you agree or disagree with this statement? Explain your position.

Jane Goodall is an animal rights activist. She began her career by studying chimpanzees in the jungles of Africa. What do you think Jane learned about chimpanzees? Write your ideas here.

_____

_____

_____

_____

Read the following passage to find out what Jane learned about chimpanzees.

© www.CartoonStock.com/Rod Jones

"I hope you feel guilty. He was an animal rights campaigner."

Jane Goodall

As a child, Jane Goodall dreamed of living with animals in Africa and writing books about them. At the age of 23, Jane left the comfort of her home and set sail for Africa. Jane arrived in Africa ready to fulfill her dreams and start her life's journey.

In 1957, Jane met a man who changed her life. The man was Dr. Louis Leaky, a well-known scientist. Dr. Leaky knew that Jane had not attended university and that she lacked training as a scientist. Yet he hired Jane to study chimpanzees because he was impressed with Jane's sharp, **inquisitive** mind and her passion for animals.

Stop and Think:

What can you conclude about Dr. Leaky?

Jane's task was to track and observe a group of chimpanzees in Africa's wild jungles. In order to study the chimps' way of life, Jane crawled through dense prickly brush and sat shivering and exhausted through torrential downpours. She made groundbreaking discoveries that proved chimps are like humans in many ways.

Stop and Think:

Think of one way that a chimpanzee is like a human. Read on to see if your idea matches the passage.

Jane watched chimps make a simple tool from a twig to catch termites. Prior to this discovery, humans believed they were the only species that made and used tools to better their lives. Jane also documented cases of chimps showing human emotion. She watched a young chimpanzee withdraw from life and die of grief

> **species:** a group of animals (or plants) with common characteristics that is able to reproduce

after its mother died. She watched chimpanzee groups go to war, not only injuring but killing one another. Jane was shocked to learn that chimps, like humans, have a dark side to their nature.

Jane's love of animals and her lack of formal training became clear in her field notes. Jane named the chimpanzees and described their characters. Because of this, many scientists dismissed Jane as an amateur. In the 1960s, scientists assigned numbers to animals and ignored their emotions. Today, like Jane, most field researchers name the animals they study.

The influence of Jane's work with and for animals began to spread beyond the world of science. In 1991, a group of 16 local teens met with Jane at her home in Tanzania. The group voiced concerns over the environment, the welfare of **domestic** animals, and the future of wild animals. With Jane's guidance, the teens educated local villagers about the humane treatment of chickens.

> **Tanzania:** a country on the east coast of Africa

Stop and Think:

Describe how you would raise chickens in a humane way.

This small project was the start of Roots & Shoots—a program for youth who want to make a better world. Today, Roots & Shoots includes tens of thousands of members in nearly 100 countries. The members work on local projects aimed at helping people, animals, and the environment.

Jane Goodall started her career as a novice field researcher. She is now one of the most influential **advocates** of animal rights. Her books, tours, and undying passion continue to inspire many.

> **humane:** causing the least amount of pain; kind

• • • • • • • • • • • • • • • •

Check the ideas you wrote on page 1 about Jane Goodall. Can you find your ideas in the passage?
> If not, do your ideas connect in some way to the ideas in the passage? How?

▶▶ Discussion

1. Do you believe it is important to learn about animals in the wild? Why or why not? If you were a field researcher, which animal would you like to study? Explain why.

2. Find three facts in the passage that show Jane was passionate about animals.

3. Describe Jane's influence on scientists and young adults.

4. A pioneer is a person who helps develop new ways of thinking and doing things. Do you think Jane was a pioneer? Explain your answer.

5. Many organizations support the humane treatment of animals. Do you think society needs these organizations? Explain your answer.

Summarizing

A summary states the central message in a piece of text. A summary includes the most important ideas in the text. It does not include details such as examples, quotes, or description. You can summarize a small piece of text, like a paragraph, or a big piece of text, like a book.

Reread paragraph 3 of the passage, on page 2.
Choose the best summary.

(a) Jane's fieldwork was hard. For example, she had to crawl through thick brush.

(b) Jane looked for chimpanzees in the wild jungles of Africa.

(c) Jane's work was hard, but she learned that chimpanzees are like humans.

Explain your choice.
   Does the summary you chose
   • contain the most important idea from each paragraph?
   • omit details such as quotes, examples, and descriptions?

Vocabulary

Circle the best meaning for each bolded word.
Figure out what the word means by looking at how it is used in the sentence.

1. My neighbour is too **inquisitive**. The other day she asked me how much money I earn.
   (a) busy; involved in many activities   (b) curious; asking lots of questions
   (c) shy or inhibited   (d) demanding or selfish

2. Horses have not always been **domestic**. Years ago, herds of wild horses ran free on the prairies.
   (a) extinct; no longer existing   (b) hard to find or track
   (c) depending on nature to survive   (d) tame; living with or near humans

3. The **advocate** for clean water demanded to know how and why the community's water had become contaminated.
   (a) person who supports causes   (b) person who breaks the law
   (c) person who is sick   (d) person who is bossy

Write an answer for each question. Use complete sentences.

1. Young children are naturally **inquisitive**. Why do you think some children lose their natural curiosity as they get older?

_____

_____

2. Many people keep **domestic** animals such as dogs, cats, and fish in their home. Why do you think having pets is so popular?

_____

_____

3. Which group of people would you like to be an **advocate** for? How could you support those people?

_____

_____

Mini-Lesson: Making Inferences

An inference is an educated guess. Imagine seeing a long lineup of people waiting to get into a department store. We can make the inference, or educated guess, that the department store is having a grand opening. Or that it is having a great sale. How did we make these inferences? We used our knowledge and experience. We know that many people love shopping and bargains.

We often make inferences about what we see. We also make inferences when we read. Why? Because the author does not always tell us, the readers, everything.

Active readers use the text together with their knowledge and experiences to figure out the author's meaning.

Look at the chart below. Make one inference for each of the observations. Explain how you were able to make the inference. The first one is an example.

Observation	My inference
A teenage boy is standing by a pay phone saying something to people as they walk by.	*I think the teenager is asking people for change to use the phone. (You need change to use a pay phone. Some people stand on the street and ask for change).*
1. A woman takes a sip of her coffee and quickly spits it out.	*I think*
2. A man runs by on the sidewalk saying, "I'm five minutes away. Love you. Bye."	*I think*

Read what the author says about Jane Goodall.
Make an inference. The first one is an example.

Text	My inference
As a child, Jane Goodall dreamed of living with animals in Africa and writing books about them.	*I think animals were more important to Jane than people.*
1. At the age of 23, Jane left the comfort of her home and set sail for Africa.	*I think*
2. In order to study the chimps' way of life, Jane crawled through dense prickly brush and sat shivering and exhausted through torrential downpours.	*I think*
3. Jane named the chimpanzees and described their characters. Today, like Jane, most field researchers name the animals they study.	*I think*

Literacy Practice: Home Page

The Internet contains millions of websites that provide information. All websites are organized in a similar way even though each contains different information. The home page, or main page, of a website lists the site's contents. The home page also provides ways to navigate, or find your way, to other pages of information in the website.

Review the home page on page 9.
Navigate the home page by answering the following questions:

1. What is name of the organization that put up this home page?

   _____

2. What would you click in the **tool bar** to

   (a) find out more about Roots & Shoots? _____ .

   (b) find a Roots & Shoots project in your community? _____ .

   (c) involve your child with Roots & Shoots? _____ .

3. Which **link** would you click in **News** and **Events** to read about

   (a) environmental programs? _____ .

   (b) bullying? _____ .

   (c) more events? _____ .

4. Which **link** would you click to buy a book about chimpanzees?

   _____

5. How many ways does the **footer** provide to contact Roots & Shoots? _____

Tool Bar: sends you to another page in the website

KIDS & TEENS • GROUP LEADERS • PARENTS • EDUCATORS • COLLEGE STUDENTS • SUPPORTERS • MEMBERS

about us | find a group | contact us | donate | store | 🛒   [   ] search

 roots&shoots The Power of Youth is Global

A program of the Jane Goodall Institute   JaneGoodall.org

human community

environment

WASTE   PAPER   CANS

animals

NEWS/EVENTS

UPDATE FROM THE FIELD: Send Messages of Hope for young people in Haiti

Roots & Shoots National Youth Leadership Council Members call on the entire Roots & Shoots Network to send Messages of Hope to youth who were victims of the earthquake in Haiti.

Learn More

NEWS

Roots & Shoots finds Green Heroes

Roots & Shoots for Andamooka

Roots & Shoots Curriculum Update

view all news

EVENTS

Chinese New Year

No Name Calling Week

Martin Luther King Jr. Day of Service

view all events

GET INVOLVED ➔
Explore all the ways you can participate in Roots & Shoots

MEMBER LOGIN

Email Address [   ]

[••••••••]

➔

☐ Remember me

Forgot your password?

NOT A MEMBER?

Sign up now. ➔
It's fast and easy!

Link: an underlined word or phrase that sends you to another page in the website

ROOTS & SHOOTS STORE   visit our store

Lessons for Hope Teachers Guide (PDF)
$14.95

Foster Care Handbook
$14.95

BeadforLife Single Bangle Bracelet
$5.00

Questions?

Footer

Email Us | **Call:** 800.592.JANE | **Write:** Roots & Shoots program, the Jane Goodall Institute, 4245 North Fairfax Drive, Suite 600, Arlington, VA 22203 USA

Dictionary Use

Mark the following statements true (T) or false (F).
Use the dictionary entries as needed.

1. A **dense** book is a good choice if you want a fun read. _____

2. It is possible to take advantage of a person who is **dense**. _____

3. A **novice** skater is probably wobbly on his feet. _____

4. **Torrential** flooding is possible after a light summer shower. _____

5. The fast food industry has the **welfare** of children in mind. _____

---

dense (adj.) **1:** crowded or packed together: THICK (*a dense fog*)
  2: SLOW-WITTED; DULL **3:** difficult to read or understand

nov-ice (n.) **1:** a new member of a religious order **2:** a person who is
  inexperienced or untrained

tor-ren-tial (adj.) coming in a large, fast stream like rushing water

wel-fare (n.) **1:** the happiness, health, and prosperity of a person or
  community **2:** government financial support for those in need of assistance

---

© CP Images

People
Dalai Lama

Vocabulary: rigorous   uprising   oppress

Mini-Lesson: Making Inferences

Literacy Practice: Political Map

© BigStockPhoto

Buddhist monks walk through a community.

▶▶ Discussion

Some religious leaders are called monks. They follow the Buddhist religion. Buddhists believe that people are reborn after death.

The Dalai Lama is a Buddhist monk. He is the spiritual leader of the Tibetan people. Tibet lies between India and China.

How do you think the Tibetan people chose the Dalai Lama to be their leader?

_____

_____

_____

Read the following passage to find out how the Dalai Lama was chosen to be the spiritual leader of Tibet.

Dalai Lama

A group of men travel across Tibet, looking for the boy. The search party follows up on every lead, which makes their mission slow and difficult. The men are Tibetan monks. They are searching for the most important person in Tibet, the Dalai Lama.

Tibetan monks surrender to the Chinese.

In 1937, during the fourth year of the search, a rainbow appears in the heavens. The monks follow the rainbow to a small hut in the high hills of Tibet. The monks enter the home and introduce themselves to a poor peasant family. The family's youngest child is a two-year-old boy named Lhamo.

The monks observe and play games with the little boy. They put Lhamo through a series of tests. Lhamo understands languages he has never heard and names objects he has never seen. Lhamo entertains the monks with stories about his past lives. The monks know their search is over; they have found the 14th Dalai Lama.

> Buddhists believe people are reborn after their death. This belief is called "reincarnation." Lhamo is the reincarnation of the 13th Dalai Lama.

Stop and Think:

How do you think Lhamo can understand languages he has never heard and name objects he has never seen?

The Dalai's life changed dramatically. He and his family moved to Lhasa, the capital of Tibet. By 1940, they were living in Potala Palace. At the age of six, the Dalai Lama began a **rigorous** education that prepared him to become the leader of Tibet. He studied languages, math, science, and history. His study of Buddhism taught him the meaning and purpose of life. The young Dalai Lama became a Buddhist scholar by the age of 24.

> **Potala Palace** (poh-tah-lah): was the main home of the Dalai Lama. The Chinese have turned the palace into a museum.

Stop and Think:

Imagine you are the young Dalai Lama. Do you enjoy your childhood? Why or why not?

sovereign: having the right to self-govern

The Dalai Lama's training prepared him to deal with China. For generations, Chinese leaders had viewed Tibet as a part of China. But Tibet had always seen itself as a sovereign nation. By the 1950s, China controlled Tibet. The Chinese suppressed the culture, language, and religion of the Tibetan people. For the first time in their history, Tibetans suffered from hunger.

Stop and Think:

Which country do you think is larger—China or Tibet? Explain your answer.

The Dalai Lama believed truth, justice, courage, and peace paved the path to freedom. But, in 1959, Tibetans revolted against Chinese rule. The Chinese crushed the **uprising** and Tibetans became victims of torture and killings. The Dalai Lama was ready to give himself up to the Chinese in exchange for the safety of his people. But the people refused and convinced him to flee to India. The Dalai Lama knew he must continue to live as Tibet's political and spiritual leader in order to give his people hope.

The Dalai Lama received the Nobel Peace Prize in 1989 for his sacrifices and efforts in promoting freedom and peace.

The Dalai Lama still lives in exile in India. He hopes to make peace with the Chinese, who continue to **oppress** his people. The Dalai Lama travels the world. He speaks about the importance of world peace and religious harmony. He spreads his message about Tibet's struggle for freedom. The world listens, and waits, for the day that the Tibetan people are once again free.

Check the ideas you wrote on page 11 about freedoms and rights. Can you find your ideas in the passage?
  If not, do your ideas connect in some way
  to the ideas in the passage? How?

▶▶ Discussion

1. The Dalai Lama believes in religious harmony. Do you believe that religious harmony is important? Why or why not? In your opinion, why are some people intolerant of different religious or spiritual beliefs?

2. Find three details in the passage that prove the Dalai Lama is important to the Tibetan people.

3. Reread paragraph 4 of the passage, on page 12. How do you know that the Dalai Lama was very intelligent?

4. Which of the following would the Dalai Lama support?
   Explain your choices.

   (a) a hunger strike (b) negotiation   (c) bombing a political office
   (d) an invasion   (e) rioting in protest (f) going to jail for a belief

5. Which groups of people in your community or country lack freedom? What type of freedom have they lost? Why have these groups of people lost these freedoms? Do you think they will regain these freedoms? Why or why not?

Summarizing

Reread paragraphs 2 and 3 of the passage, on page 12.
Choose the best summary.

(a) The Buddhist monks find a young boy named Lhamo. The monks believe Lhamo is the Dalai Lama. The monks test Lhamo. The tests prove he is the 14th Dalai Lama.

(b) The Buddhist monks find a young boy living with his peasant family. The family live in a small hut high in the hills.

(c) The Buddhist monks find a young boy that they believe is the Dalai Lama. His name is Lhamo. The monks play games with Lhamo.

Explain your choice.
   Does the summary you chose
     • contain the most important idea from each paragraph?
     • omit details such as quotes, examples, and descriptions?

Vocabulary

Circle the best meaning for each bolded word.
Figure out what the word means by looking at how it is used in the sentence.

1. The course was **rigorous**. I had three hours of homework every night and a major
   test once a week. I worked really hard just to pass.
   (a) expensive   (b) disorganized
   (c) fun and easy to do   (d) strict and demanding

2. The **uprising** led to the overthrow of the corrupt government. However, over
   500 people lost their lives as they fought the government's army.
   (a) election   (b) peaceful protest
   (c) rebellion   (d) obeying of unpopular laws

3. One way governments **oppress** people is by not allowing free elections.
   (a) help or encourage   (b) collect money from
   (c) control with cruel injustice   (d) give a lot of freedom to

Write an answer for each question. Use complete sentences.

1. Some exercise programs involve a lot of sweating, grunting, and pain. Name two
   activities that might be included in a **rigorous** exercise program.

   _____

   _____

2. The news often has stories of **uprisings** in poor countries. Give two reasons why
   people might rebel against their government.

   _____

   _____

3. For a long time, women were **oppressed** in the workplace. They were hired for the
   dead-end jobs and were paid less than men for doing the same work. Have women
   achieved equality in the workplace? Explain your answer.

   _____

   _____

Mini-Lesson: Making Inferences

The author does not always tell readers everything. Readers need to make inferences, or educated guesses about the author's meaning. Readers use their knowledge and experiences together with the text.

Read what the author says about the Dalai Lama. Make an inference. The first one is an example.

Text	My inference
In 1937, during the fourth year of the search, a rainbow appears in the heavens. The monks follow the rainbow to a small hut in the high hills of Tibet.	*I think the monks believe in a higher power, which is guiding them on their mission. That's why they follow the rainbow.*
1. The Chinese suppressed the culture, language, and religion of the Tibetan people.	*I think*
2. The Dalai Lama was ready to give himself up to the Chinese in exchange for the safety of his people.	*I think*
3. The Dalai Lama still lives in exile in India.	*I think*

Good Samaritans are everyday people who perform simple acts of kindness for strangers. Read the following story. Who are the good Samaritans?

My children were young at the time—four years old and the other only a year and a half. I sold my car so I could fly us home. The car would not have survived a long winter drive. My mom had a small room that me and the kids could sleep in.

Buying Christmas gifts was out of the question that year. I went through my mom's closet and found, buried against the back wall, two of my old Barbies. One for each of the kids. My son was so young I figured he wouldn't know the difference.

I called a charity, but it was already Christmas Eve. I told them about the Barbie dolls. If I could just get some Barbie accessories for the dolls, I explained, I could make Christmas special. The man on the phone said he was sorry, but it was so late that there was nothing he could do.

Late that night, my mom and I were huddled under a blanket drinking hot tea and watching TV. The buzzer rang. To my surprise, people came in with boxes of Barbie stuff and even had gifts for my son. I just cried!

Since that Christmas, I always make sure that we do something to make Christmas special for at least one family that could use a little cheer.

Read the story again. Underline the sentences in the story that match these inferences.

1. The writer's car was not new.

2. The writer did not have much money.

3. The writer's mom had lived in the same place for many years.

4. The writer's son was a year and a half old.

5. It was cold in the room.

6. The writer was touched by the kindness of strangers.

Literacy Practice: Political Map

Maps provide a lot of information. The main purpose of political maps is to show boundaries. For example, they show boundaries between countries and provinces. Like all maps, they also show direction and distance.

When reading a map, pay attention to the title, any insets, the key, the compass, and the scale.

Use the map on the following page to answer these questions:

1. What is the **title** of the map? _____

2. Look at the **inset**. What information does it give you?

   _____

3. (a) How are international boundaries shown in the **key**? _____

   (b) Write the names of four countries that border China.

   _____   _____   _____   _____

4. (a) How are provincial boundaries shown in the key? _____

   (b) How many provinces does China have?

   (i) about 5   (ii) about 15   (iii) more than 15

5. What is the capital city of India? _____

6. Where is China in relation to India? Use the **compass**.

   (a) southeast   (b) northwest   (c) southwest   (d) northeast

7. Use the **scale** to estimate the distance between

   (a) Harbin and Hong Kong   (i) 1,000 km (ii) 5,000 km   (iii) 10,000 km

   (b) the capital cities of China and India   (i) 5,000 km (ii) 10,000 km (iii) 15,000 km

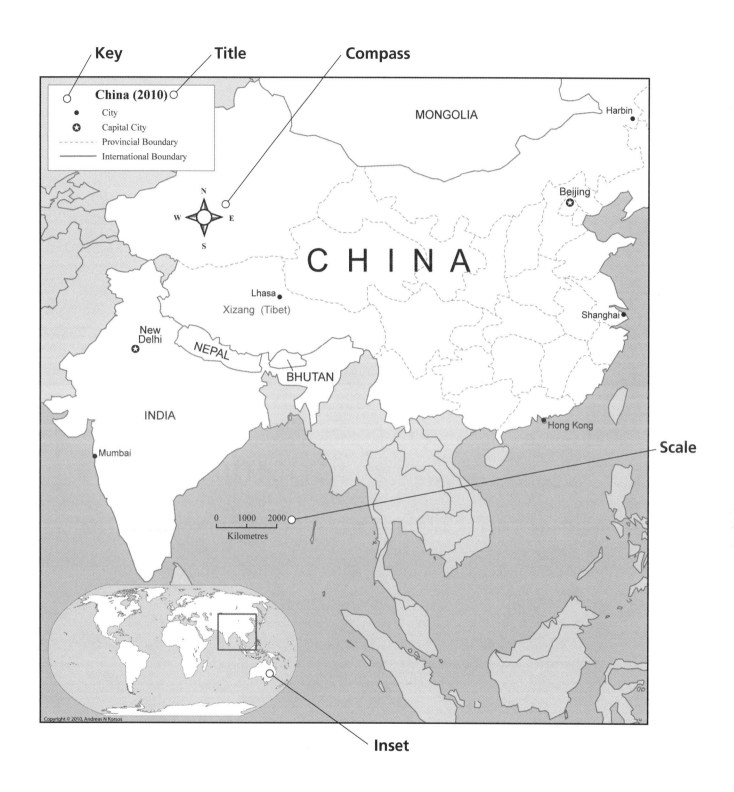

Key　　**Title**　　**Compass**

China (2010)
- City
- Capital City
- Provincial Boundary
- International Boundary

MONGOLIA

Harbin

N
W　E
S

Beijing

CHINA

Lhasa
Xizang (Tibet)

Shanghai

New
Delhi

NEPAL

BHUTAN

INDIA

Hong Kong

Scale

Mumbai

0　1000　2000
Kilometres

Copyright © 2010, Andreas N Korsos

Inset

Dictionary Use

Mark the following statements true (T) or false (F).
Use the dictionary entries as needed.

1. People would probably **revolt** against a drop in food prices. _____

2. One way to **revolt** is to follow the rules and say nothing. _____

3. A **sovereign** was probably round, like a quarter. _____

4. Two-year-olds can **suppress** anger. _____

5. You might **suppress** a yawn to show you are not bored. _____

---

re-volt (n.) **1:** violent action against a ruler or government: REBELLION **2:** something that shows you will not be controlled or influenced *(a revolt against high food prices)*

re-volt (v.) REBEL

sov-er-eign (n.) **1:** a king or queen **2:** an old British gold coin

sov-er-eign (adj.) **1:** having unlimited power or authority *(the sovereign power of a queen)* **2:** having the right to self-govern: INDEPENDENT **3:** highest and most important *(The sovereign duty of a government is to protect the people.)*

sup-press (v.) **1:** to end or stop something by force **2:** to not allow people to see or know about something *(suppress a news story)* **3:** to stop yourself from feeling or doing something *(suppress anger; suppress a smile)* **4:** to slow or stop the growth, development, or normal functioning of something *(The diet pills suppress your appetite.)*

Relationships
Bullying

Vocabulary: retaliate   intervention   diversity

Mini-Lesson: Finding the Main Idea

Literacy Practice: Diversity in Ads

"SAY AREN'T YOU THE DOG THAT USED TO CHASE ME AROUND THE BLOCK?"

▶▶ Discussion

Bullying is a growing concern in schools across North America.

Do you think bullying is a serious issue? Why or why not?

Some students become the target of bullies; others do not. Why do you think some students are targeted more than others by bullies?

_____

_____

_____

_____

Read the following passage to find out why some children become the target of bullies.

Bullying

Dana's mom was getting annoyed with her. She always seemed to be losing things. At first it was her school supplies. Then it was her math book. When Dana came home one day without her glasses, her mom decided to look into the matter. She found out that, like many students, Dana had become the target of a bully.

Why, like Dana, are some children targeted by bullies? At its root, bullying is the strong preying on the weak. Children who lack friends, social skills, or self-confidence are easy targets for bullies. These children, who tend to be shy or submissive, do not stick up for themselves. Bullies also pick on children that they see as being different. Being different could mean having a disability or belonging to a minority group. It could also mean wearing the "wrong" clothes, being too smart, or just being thin with freckles. Bullied children who feel they are different believe they deserve to be picked on.

In Canada and the US, 15 percent of students fall victim to bullying.

Bullied children fear that parents and teachers cannot protect them from bullies. Or that adults will just say, "Ignore them" or "Fight back." In many cases, bullies will **retaliate** if their victims speak out. So, many victims of bullying stay silent.

Stop and Think:

What are some other warning signs that a child is being bullied?

Bullying thrives on silence, but adults can spot the warning signs. Bullied children might show signs of sudden physical change such as losing weight or always looking tired. Bullied children may get stomach aches and headaches. They may lose their appetites or go through mood swings. Signs of fear or worry such as refusing to take the school bus or losing interest in friends need follow-up. Torn clothing or missing possessions can signal trouble, as in Dana's case.

Dealing with bullying can be difficult. **Intervention** by adults may worsen relationships between bullies and their victims. But parents of bullied children can turn to school authorities for help. Teachers can provide more supervision in hallways and playgrounds. Principals can talk with the parents of bullies. Many schools have anti-bullying programs in place and welcome parents' input.

Stop and Think:

Imagine you had a child who was being bullied. How would you help your child? Read on to see if your ideas match the passage.

Parents can also access youth and community centres. These centres often have youth workers who can provide anti-bullying strategies.

Parents can help a bullied child in different ways. Let the child know that bullying is not acceptable and that difference and **diversity** should be celebrated. Teach the child how to use "self-talk," which is a silent pep talk one can use when feeling picked on. Help the child develop skills for making friends, such as how to share, compromise, and handle conflict. Encouraging the child to pursue a favourite hobby such as drawing or martial arts can help the child build self-confidence.

Stop and Think:

Describe a time when you talked to yourself, or used self-talk, to get through an anxious moment.

Self-talk examples:

It's okay to be different.

I have a right to be here.

I am a nice person.

The consequences of growing up as a victim of bullying can be severe. Immediate, but thoughtful, solutions are needed at the first sign that a child may be a victim of bullying.

· · · · · · · · · · · · · · · · · ·

Check the ideas you wrote on page 21 about bullying.
Can you find your ideas in the passage?
　　　If not, do your ideas connect in some way
　　　to the ideas in the passage? How?

▶▶ Discussion

1. Bullying thrives on silence. Have you ever witnessed bullying and remained silent? Why might someone remain silent when witnessing bullying?

2. Find three reasons in the passage that explain why bullied children remain silent.

3. What advice does the passage offer on (a) who can help bullied children and (b) how they can help?

4. In your opinion, what effects might the code of silence have on

   (a) bullied children?   (b) the bullies?   (c) parents?

5. Sometimes adults are victims of bullying in the workplace. What are some examples of physical bullying in the workplace? What are some examples of emotional bullying? Is one type of bullying worse than the other? Explain your answer.

Summarizing

Reread paragraphs 4 and 5 of the passage, on pages 22 and 23. Choose the best summary.

(a) Parents can tell if a child is being bullied by looking for warning signs. For example, Dana seemed to be losing her possessions all the time.

(b) Sudden physical or emotional changes in a child can warn a parent that the child is being bullied. Parents and educators can work together to help the child.

(c) Bullied children stay silent. However, parents can turn to school authorities for help.

Explain your choice.
   Does the summary you chose
      • contain the most important idea from each paragraph?
      • omit details such as quotes, examples, and descriptions?

Vocabulary

Circle the best meaning for each bolded word.
Figure out what the word means by looking at how it is used in the sentence.

1. He found out his girlfriend was dishonest. He **retaliated** by cutting up all her family photos.
   (a) congratulated
   (b) became confused
   (c) told the truth
   (d) got revenge; attacked in return

2. The garbage strike lasted for weeks. It came to an end only after government **intervention**. The government forced the workers off the picket line.
   (a) support
   (b) involvement
   (c) destruction
   (d) funding; giving money

3. The **diversity** of cultures in my community is great. I have neighbours who have come from all over the world.
   (a) equality
   (b) variety
   (c) weakness
   (d) advantage

Write an answer for each question. Use complete sentences.

1. Some children **retaliate** when faced with conflict. Suggest one positive way a child can respond to conflict.

   _____

   _____

2. Some people are nervous about any kind of medical treatment. Give two reasons why people might have or develop a fear of medical **intervention**.

   _____

   _____

3. People have different values and beliefs due to culture, religion, and upbringing. What can parents do to teach their children to celebrate **diversity** among people?

   _____

   _____

Mini-Lesson: Finding the Main Idea

The main idea is the most important idea in the paragraph. It consists of two parts: (1) the topic of the paragraph, and (2) the main point the author makes about the topic. The main idea is often stated clearly in a paragraph.

Read the paragraph below.
Underline the main idea.

> Bullying thrives on silence, but adults can spot the warning signs. Bullied children might show show signs of sudden physical change such as losing weight or always looking tired. They may get stomach aches and headaches. They may lose their appetites or go through mood swings. Signs of fear or worry such as refusing to take the school bus or losing interest in friends need follow-up. Torn clothing or missing possessions can signal trouble, as in Dana's case.

Did you underline "adults can spot the warning signs"? The topic is warning signs of bullying. The main point the author makes about warning signs is that adults can spot them.

One way to check if you have identified the main idea is to find supporting details.

Read the paragraph again.
Find three other details that support the main idea.

1. *Bullied children lose weight quickly.*

2. _____

3. _____

4. _____

Read the paragraphs on the following page.
Underline the main ideas. List supporting details.

Paragraph 1

Dealing with bullying can be difficult. Intervention by adults may worsen relationships between bullies and their victims. But parents of bullied children can turn to school authorities for help. Teachers can provide more supervision in hallways and playgrounds. Principals can talk with the parents of bullies. Many schools have anti-bullying programs in place and welcome parents' input.

Supporting Details:

1. _____

2. _____

3. _____

Paragraph 2

Parents can help a bullied child in different ways. Let the child know that bullying is not acceptable and that difference and diversity should be celebrated. Teach the child how to use "self-talk," which is a silent pep talk one can use when feeling picked on. Help the child develop skills for making friends, such as how to share, compromise, and handle conflict. Encouraging the child to pursue a favourite hobby such as drawing or martial arts can help the child build self-confidence.

Supporting Details:

1. _____

2. _____

3. _____

4. _____

Active readers take note of main ideas and supporting details as they read. Knowing how ideas relate to one another helps readers understand the ideas.

Literacy Practice: Diversity in Ads

Ads are a part of everyday life. But do ads reflect everyday life in your world?

Effective ads respect the diversity of Canada's population. Some ads attract a specific audience such as sports fans, seniors, or parents of young children. Other ads reach as broad an audience as possible.

Look at the three photos.
Imagine you have to choose one of the photos
for an ad promoting a family day in your province or territory.
Write down how each photo reflects your everyday life.
Choose the winning photo for the family day ad.

Photo 1

How Photo 1 reflects my life:

_____

_____

_____

_____

Photo 2

How Photo 2 reflects my life:

_____

_____

_____

_____

Photo 3

© iStockphoto/naphtalina.com

How Photo 3 reflects my life:

_____

_____

_____

_____

_____

The best photo for the Family Day ad is _____.

But I suggest the following changes to make the photo reflect my everyday life more:

_____

_____

▶▶ Discussion

Think about an ad you have seen recently.

In what ways does the ad reflect your world?

In what ways does the ad reflect someone else's world?

And what do you think?

In the past two decades, female bullying has risen dramatically in Canada. Girls use psychological tactics when they bully. For example, they shun, tease, or spread vicious rumours about their victims.

Dictionary Use

Mark the following statements true (T) or false (F).
Use the dictionary entries as needed.

1. Going to jail for one year for committing murder is a **severe** punishment. _____

2. One **severe** effect of not getting enough sleep is feeling a little tired. _____

3. **Severe** clothing is suitable at a funeral. _____

4. **Submissive** dogs bark, growl, and jump up on people. _____

5. A **submissive** student might stop going to class rather than telling the teacher the course is too easy. _____

---

se-vere (adj.) **1:** very bad or unpleasant *(severe pain)* **2:** very strict or formal *(a severe leader)* **3:** requiring great effort *(a severe challenge)* **4:** having little decoration: PLAIN *(a severe hairstyle)*

sub-mis-sive (adj.) **1:** OBEDIENT **2:** showing that one will usually back down

---

Relationships
Women in Gangs

Vocabulary: lavish   infiltrate   secluded

Mini-Lesson: Finding the Main Idea

Literacy Practice: Map

"You wanna join the gang, stupid? Then get rid of that dumb collar!"

▶▶ Discussion

In 2006, the Criminal Intelligence Service Canada (CISC) filed a report on organized crime. The report stated that 11,000 people across Canada were members of a gang or connected to a gang.

(a) What percentage of gang members do you think are female? _____

(b) Why do you think females join gangs? Write your ideas here.

_____

_____

_____

_____

Read the following passage to find out how many females join gangs, and why.

Women in Gangs

The offer from Sandi's drug dealer was too good to resist. An all-expenses paid weekend in Miami, plus $5,000 in cash when she returned to Canada. Two trips later, Sandi and her son moved into a safer community. The catch? Sandi had to smuggle cocaine into Canada. The result? Sandi soon became a full member of her dealer's street gang.

In North America, about 8 percent of gang members are females. Like Sandi, many females turn to gangs for money and protection. These young women have usually grown up in rough, lower-income neighbourhoods. They live in constant fear of street violence. In many cases, a single adult heads the family, which is often coping with money, health, or legal issues. The young women want to escape from a life of physical, emotional, or sexual abuse. A gang appears to be a safe haven from the violence in their lives.

Gangs also offer females a source of income and a **lavish** lifestyle full of trips, sports cars, and designer clothes. Being part of a gang opens the door to the underground economy. Many undereducated females feel that joining the underground economy is one sure way to make money and get ahead.

> **underground economy:** includes any money-making activity that is illegal or not recorded for tax purposes

Stop and Think:

What underground activities do you think female gangsters are involved in? Read on to see if your ideas match the passage.

The same gang that offers safety and money also uses their female members as a source of sex, income, and information. Many females are forced into a life of prostitution. Or they take part in property theft such as shoplifting and robbery. There is a growing belief that gangs now recruit females to commit electronic theft. A young girl who has a low-wage job in a clothing store, for example, is an ideal candidate to commit credit card fraud.

Stop and Think:

Why do you think this young girl is an ideal candidate to commit credit card fraud?

Many gangs use female members as "drug mules." The women smuggle drugs across borders and through security checks in creative ways. Sometimes, they swallow plastic bags or capsules filled with a drug, most often cocaine. The risk lies not only in being caught but in dying from cocaine poisoning if a capsule or plastic bag bursts.

Stop and Think:

Do you think the benefits of being a gang member outweigh the risks?

Female gangsters also trade sex for information. These young girls **infiltrate** rival gangs and seduce the gang members to find out about drug deals or the movements of key gang leaders. They also seduce witnesses to gang crimes in order to find out how much the witnesses may know. If a witness knows too much, the young girls lure him, or her, to a **secluded** place to be beaten or killed.

The promise of security is hard to resist for low-income women who lack education and come from violent backgrounds. For these women, the hope for a better life outweighs the risks of being a gang member.

• • • • • • • • • • • • • • • • •

Check the ideas you wrote on page 31 about gangs.
Can you find your ideas in the passage?
If not, do your ideas connect in some way to the ideas in the passage? How?

▶▶ Discussion

1. Sometimes, people have to make hard choices in their lives. What are some examples of hard choices people have to make? What helps people make these choices?

2. Find three reasons in the passage that explain why women join gangs.

3. Do male gang members respect female gang members? Support your answer with details from the passage.

4. Research shows that the number of all-female gangs is increasing. Why do you think some women form their own gangs?

5. What can parents do to prevent their children from joining gangs? How can parents tell if their teenager has joined a gang? What should parents do if they suspect their teenager has joined a gang?

Summarizing

**Reread paragraphs 5 and 6 of the passage, on page 33.
Choose the best summary.**

(a) Female gang members smuggle cocaine across borders by putting the drug in plastic bags, which they swallow.

(b) Female gang members smuggle cocaine. They also get information from people who witness gang crimes.

(c) Female gang members are used as drug mules. They also gather information for their gang, often by using sex.

Explain your choice.
    Does the summary you chose
        • contain the most important idea from each paragraph?
        • omit details such as quotes, examples, and descriptions?

Vocabulary

Circle the best meaning for each bolded word.
Figure out what the word means by looking at how it is used in the sentence.

1. The parents put on a **lavish** birthday party when their daughter turned 16. They rented a big hall, invited over 200 guests, and hired three dance bands.
   (a) not on time; not dependable
   (b) having a rich or expensive quality
   (c) causing great joy
   (d) less than expected

2. It was possible to **infiltrate** the organization because there were no security checks in place.
   (a) secretly enter or join
   (b) election
   (c) rebellion
   (d) obeying of unpopular laws

3. She parked the car in a **secluded** area of the thick woods. Only the occasional chirp of a lonely bird broke the silence.
   (a) with wide open spaces
   (b) full of quick movement
   (c) hidden from view; not used by many
   (d) under construction

Write an answer for each question. Use complete sentences.

1. Some young couples go into debt because they spend thousands of dollars on a **lavish** wedding. Do you think it is important to have a big wedding? Why or why not?

   _____

   _____

2. Police work often involves danger. For example, police risk being discovered and killed when they go undercover and **infiltrate** drug rings. What two other activities put police at risk?

   _____

   _____

3. Many neighbourhoods have spaces that are **secluded** or abandoned, such as empty lots or old buildings. One way to make a space more people-friendly is to use it as a community garden. How else can abandoned neighbourhood spaces be used?

   _____

   _____

Mini-Lesson: Finding the Main Idea

The main idea is the most important idea in the paragraph. The main idea is often stated clearly in the paragraph. Sometimes, however, the main idea is not stated; it is implied. The reader has to figure out the main idea. One way to figure out the main idea is by asking, "What is the **most important thing** the author wants me to learn from this paragraph?"

Read the following paragraph.
Choose the correct main idea.

> The offer from Sandi's drug dealer was too good to resist. An all-expenses paid weekend in Miami, plus $5,000 in cash when she returned to Canada. Two trips later, Sandi and her son moved into a safer community. The catch? Sandi had to smuggle cocaine into Canada. The result? Sandi soon became a full member of her dealer's street gang.

(a) For some, the hope for a better life outweighs the risks of joining a gang.

(b) Sandi was able to live in a safer community.

(c) Sandi became a full member of her dealer's street gang.

Did you choose (a)? If yes, you are right! The author uses Sandi's experience as an example to show that joining a gang is risky, but hard to resist, because of the chance to make a lot of money.

One way to check if you have identified the main idea is to find supporting details.

Read the paragraph again.
Find two details that support the main idea.

1. _____

2. _____

Read the following paragraphs.
Choose the correct main ideas. List supporting details.

Paragraph 1   Female gangsters infiltrate rival gangs and seduce the gang members to find out about drug deals or the movements of key gang leaders. They also seduce witnesses to gang crimes in order to find out how much the witnesses may know. If a witness knows too much, the young girls lure him, or her, to a secluded place to be beaten or killed.

(a) Witnesses to gang crimes can be male or female.

(b) Female gangsters trade sex for information.

(c) Gangs kill members from other gangs.

Supporting Details:

1. _____

2. _____

Paragraph 2   The most powerful members in a gang are called OGs—original gang members. OGs are well respected by the other members of the gang. They often act as mentors to new or younger gang members. Some gang members are lookouts. They watch out for police during drug deals, for example. Gang members who do the dirty work of gangs are called flunkies. They have little power in the gang and follow orders obediently. Flunkies do what they are told.

(a) OGs are the most respected gang members.

(b) Gang members have strange names.

(c) Gangs are organized, with each member having specific responsibilities.

Supporting Details:

1. _____

2. _____

3. _____

Literacy Practice: Map

Maps provide different kinds of information. Political maps, for example, show borders. Maps can also show information such as population distribution, weather patterns, or the locations of mountains, prairies, and deserts.

The following map shows the distribution of street gangs in Canada. Use the map to answer the questions below.

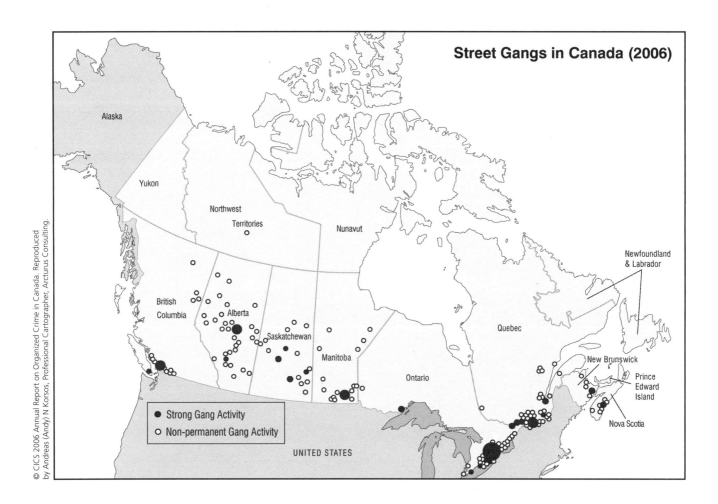

1. What do the white circles on the map represent? _____

2. What do the black circles on the map represent? _____

3. Why do the black circles vary in size? _____

RELATIONSHIPS

4. The map is based on information from 2006. Do you think the map accurately represents the location of street gangs in Canada today? Explain your answer.

_____

_____

5. (a) Where is the heaviest concentration of permanent gang activity in Canada?

   (i) northern Canada   (ii) Alberta   (iii) southern Ontario and Quebec

   (b) Why do you think so many gangs take root in this area?

   _____

   _____

   (c) Which province has the most non-permanent gang activity? _____

   Why do you think some gangs operate only temporarily, then disappear?

   _____

   _____

   (d) Why do you think there are next to no gangs in northern Canada?

   _____

   _____

6. Put an X on the map to show the location of your city or hometown. Look at the relative locations of gangs and where you live. Does the location of gangs surprise you? Or is it what you expected? Explain your answer.

_____

_____

And what do you think?

The fastest growing segment of the prison population around the world is women. Their crimes are directly linked to cuts in social programs, poor wages, and lack of education.

Dictionary Use

Mark the following statements true (T) or false (F).
Use the **dictionary entries** as needed.

1. A friend's home can be a **haven**. _____

2. Ships probably use open oceans as a **haven** from lightning storms. _____

3. When an argument comes to a **head**, it's best to remain calm. _____

4. A big company would be happy to share secrets with a **rival**. _____

5. Hockey **rivals** baseball in terms of numbers of fans. _____

---

ha-ven (n.) **1:** a harbour or port **2:** a place where you are protected from danger

head (n.) **1:** the upper part of the body that contains the mouth, the brain, and sense organs **2:** mental ability, mind, intellect (*She adds up numbers in her head.*) **3:** the position of being a leader (*head of the department*) **4:** the point when a situation becomes serious (*The discussion came to a head.*) **5:** the end of something that looks like a head in shape or position (*head of the bed*)

head (v.) **1:** to be the leader of something **2:** to go to a specific place (*head toward the kitchen*) **3:** to hit a ball with your head (*head the soccer ball into the goal*)

ri-val (n.) **1:** a person, team, etc., that tries to defeat or be more successful than another (*The two hockey teams are bitter rivals.*) **2:** someone or something almost as good as another person or thing (*the latest cell phone has no rivals*)

ri-val (v.) **rivalled; rivalling** to be as good as another person or thing (*my garden rivals the city gardens*)

Health
Insomnia

Vocabulary: chronic   decline   susceptible

Mini-Lesson: Drawing Conclusions

Literacy Practice: Medicine Label

▶▶ Discussion

Think of three adult friends or family members. According to statistics, one of these three adults may suffer from insomnia, the inability to sleep well.

Some people suffer from insomnia night after night. How does insomnia affect people in their daily lives? Write your ideas here.

"Was I snoring again?"

_____

_____

_____

_____

Read the following passage to find out how insomnia affects people's lives.

Insomnia

Sonya crawls into bed by ten and is asleep before her head hits the pillow. The next sound she hears is the ringing of an alarm clock. Sonya drags herself out of bed and through the rest of the day. She wonders why, after a full night's sleep, she feels so utterly tired.

We all know the frustration of not being able to fall asleep, or of waking up at 3:00 a.m., our minds racing. On any given night, one in three adults across North America experiences insomnia. Many suffer from insomnia because of daily stress due to concerns over paying bills, for example, or conflict with a family member. Stress can result in temporary insomnia, which lasts from a single night to a few weeks.

Stop and Think:

Have you ever experienced insomnia? What caused it?

But some people, like Sonya, suffer from **chronic** insomnia, which lasts months or even years. Chronic insomnia can be caused by medical conditions such as asthma. Or it can be caused by mental health conditions such as depression and anxiety.

Sleeping disorders such as snoring, tooth grinding, or leg jerking also lead to chronic insomnia. Sleeping disorders cause a person to wake up for a few moments again and again throughout the night. Many people, like Sonya, are not aware that they are constantly waking up. They wonder why they always feel tired. Many blame their hectic lives for their fatigue. To make matters worse, people with chronic insomnia do not believe their fatigue is worth mentioning to a health care provider. Instead, they may rely on caffeine or afternoon naps to stay alert.

anxiety: condition which results in extreme worry over everyday situations or events

Stop and Think:

In your opinion, why don't people take their fatigue seriously?

If not attended to, chronic insomnia often leads to a general **decline** in quality of life. Long periods of insomnia sap energy and affect mood. Tired people often feel irritable and less able to cope with the daily stresses of life. They may lash out at family and friends. On the job, fatigue can lead to slower reaction times and mistakes in judgment. More accidents occur. At school, fatigue affects one's ability to concentrate, learn, and remember. Fatigue also leaves people more **susceptible** to illness.

Stop and Think:

How does fatigue affect you?

People with chronic insomnia are desperate for a good night's sleep. Rather than seeing a doctor, many people self-medicate with alcohol or over-the-counter drugs. While this is a quick fix, self-medication does not get to the root cause of the problem. Discussing sleep concerns with a health care provider can lead to the right diagnosis and treatment. For some, the treatment may lead to lifestyle changes. For others, the treatment may result in counselling for depression or anxiety.

A good night's sleep is vital for health and well-being. People like Sonya who suffer from lack of sleep need to give insomnia—and its underlying causes—the attention it deserves.

In the year 2000, Canadian doctors filled out 15.7 million prescriptions for tranquillizers. This number represents almost half the entire population of Canada.

Check the ideas you wrote on page 41 about insomnia.
Can you find your ideas in the passage?
> If not, do your ideas connect in some way to the ideas in the passage? How?

▶▶ Discussion

1. Think about a family member or friend that suffers (or has suffered) from insomnia. How does insomnia affect their life? How have they tried to cure their insomnia? Have they consulted a doctor? If yes, how did the doctor help? If not, why not?

2. The passage mentions three ways that people try to cope with insomnia. What are the three ways?

3. Compare temporary and chronic insomnia. Consider (a) how long they last and (b) their causes.

4. People who suffer from insomnia often self-medicate because they are desperate for a good night's sleep. Why else might some people with insomnia self-medicate (rather than seeing a health care provider)?

5. Drinking less coffee is one lifestyle change that can reduce insomnia. What other lifestyle changes can help reduce insomnia?

Summarizing

**Reread paragraphs 5 and 6 of the passage, on page 43.
Choose the best summary.**

(a) Chronic insomnia affects a person's daily life at home, school, and work. Many sufferers self-medicate, but seeing a health care provider is a better choice.

(b) Chronic insomnia can affect relationships with family and friends. Some people self-medicate; others talk to a health care provider.

(c) Chronic insomnia can lead to a decline in the general quality of life. Some sufferers rely on alcohol for a quick fix.

Explain your choice.
   Does the summary you chose
      • contain the most important idea from each paragraph?
      • omit details such as quotes, examples, and descriptions?

Vocabulary

Circle the best meaning for each bolded word.

Figure out what the word means by looking at how it is used in the sentence.

1. He was a **chronic** complainer. Nothing ever satisfied him.
   - (a) secret; hidden from the public
   - (b) easy to please
   - (c) forgetful
   - (d) lasting a long time; happening again and again

2. The **decline** of the neighbourhood began when gangs took control of the streets. People felt unsafe and wanted to move away.
   - (a) improvement
   - (b) need to spend money
   - (c) gradual loss in quality or condition
   - (d) good reputation

3. Older people are more **susceptible** to extreme weather than younger people.
   - (a) attracted to
   - (b) made strong by
   - (c) happy with
   - (d) easily harmed or influenced by

Write an answer for each question. Use complete sentences.

1. Some people seem to have a need to lie all the time. Why do you think some people are **chronic** liars?

   _____

   _____

2. Sometimes a country's economy slows down, or goes into **decline**. How does a slow economy affect people?

   _____

   _____

3. Colds and flus spread quickly from one person to the next. What makes people **susceptible** to colds and flus?

   _____

   _____

Mini-Lesson: Drawing Conclusions

What is a conclusion?

A conclusion is a decision based on two or more facts. Active readers compare or combine facts to draw conclusions as they read.

Read the following three facts:

People with insomnia blame their hectic lives for their fatigue.

They may rely on caffeine or afternoon naps to stay alert.

They may self-medicate with alcohol or over-the-counter drugs.

What conclusion can you draw about people with insomnia?

(a) They depend on their own methods to treat their insomnia.

(b) They have had negative experiences with doctors.

Did you choose (a)? If yes, you are right. Two of the facts mention self-treatments. None of the facts gives any information about addictions or prior experiences with doctors.

Review the bar graph on the following page. Use the bar graph to fill in the percentage for each fact below. Then choose the correct conclusion for each set of facts.

Facts

1. (a) _____ percent of women consume drinks with caffeine.

   (b) _____ percent of women eat foods that are high in sugar or carbohydrates.

   (c) _____ percent of women use medication.

Conclusion: (a) Most women deal with feeling sleepy in positive ways.

(b) Most women do not use medication to deal with feeling sleepy.

Facts

2. (a) _____ percent of women do less during the day.

    (b) _____ percent of women eat foods that are high in sugar or carbohydrates.

    (c) _____ percent of women take a nap.

Conclusion: (a) Sleepiness may put some women at risk of gaining weight.

(b) Women who are overweight sleep a lot.

Facts

3. (a) _____ percent of women go to bed earlier that night.

    (b) _____ percent of women sleep more on the weekend.

    (c) _____ percent of women take a nap.

Conclusion: (a) Some women deal with feeling sleepy by getting up later.

(b) Napping is the least popular way of catching up on sleep.

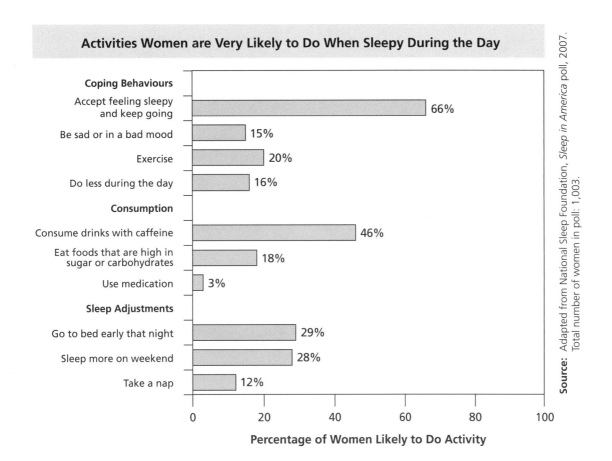

Activities Women are Very Likely to Do When Sleepy During the Day

Source: Adapted from National Sleep Foundation, *Sleep in America* poll, 2007. Total number of women in poll: 1,003.

Literacy Practice: Medicine Label

People buy over-the-counter medicines all the time. One way to learn about medicine is to read the medicine label. The medicine label gives information such as who can take the medicine, how to take the medicine safely, and possible side effects. All medicines must have a label. This is the law.

> Consumers are responsible for learning about the medicines they buy.

The medicine label to the right gives information for a lemon drink that treats colds and flu. Which sections of the label provide information about the following items?

Put the correct number in each blank.

1. side effects _____

2. dosage _____

3. storing the medicine _____

4. who *cannot* take the medicine _____

5. number of days you can take the medicine _____

6. important warnings _____

7. dealing with an overdose _____

a — **Directions for Use:** Adults and children over 12 years old: Dissolve the contents of one pouch in 225 mL (8 oz) of boiling water. Sweeten to taste if desired. May be repeated every 4-6 hours. Do not exceed 4 doses in 24 hours. It is hazardous to exceed maximum dose unless advised by a physician.

b — **Caution: This package contains enough drug to seriously harm a child. Keep out of reach of children.** In case of overdose, contact a physician or poison control centre immediately, even if there are no symptoms.

c — **Side effects:** May cause drowsiness, rash, or itching.

d — **Precautions:** Avoid alcoholic beverages, sedatives, and tranquillizers. Do not take if currently taking inhibitor drugs. Do not drive or engage in activities that require alertness.

Individuals with any medical condition of the heart, kidney or liver, high blood pressure, diabetes, allergies, asthma, or alcoholism, or the elderly, pregnant women, and nursing mothers, should take only after consultation with a doctor or pharmacist.

e — Consult a physician if underlying condition requires continued use for more than 5 days (pain), 3 days (fever), 2 days (sore throat), 1 week (cough).

f — **Storage:** Store in a cool, dry place.

Questions? 1-888-788-8181

Use the medicine label to answer the following questions:

1. You take one dose of the lemon drink at the following times: 6:00 a.m., 11:00 a.m., 3:00 p.m., and 7:00 p.m. When can you take the next dose? Explain your answer.

_____

2. You start taking the lemon drink on Wednesday night because you have a flu and fever. Friday morning, you still have the fever. Should you be concerned? Why or why not?

_____

3. (a) Should you eat before taking the lemon drink?   *Yes   No   Don't know*

   (b) What can you do to get this information?

_____

4. (a) You want to buy the lemon drink for your son, who has a sore throat. You do not have time to read the label. List three questions you should ask the pharmacist before you buy the lemon drink.

_____

_____

_____

   (b) You ask a pharmacist about giving the lemon drink to your father. List three questions the pharmacist should ask you about your father before giving advice.

_____

_____

_____

And what do you think?

Many people think that over-the-counter drugs are safe because they do not require a prescription. However, over-the-counter drugs can be addictive.

Dictionary Use

Mark the following statements true (T) or false (F).
Use the dictionary entries as needed.

1. You should get advice from a **sap.** _____

2. **Saps** are used by people when they ride a horse. _____

3. Daisies have **sap.** _____

4. A tent is an example of a **temporary** shelter. _____

5. Some partners struggle in their relationship. One **underlying** cause might
   be the way they deal with conflict. _____

---

sap (n.) **1:** a watery liquid of sugars and mineral salts inside a plant,
necessary for the plant's growth **2:** a foolish person **3:** a tunnel or trench
used by attackers to approach a protected area

sap (v.) **sapped; sapping** weaken or destroy little by little *(The flu sapped his
strength.)*

tem-po-rar-y (adj.) **1:** not permanent **2:** intended to be used for a limited
period of time *(temporary work)*

un-der-ly-ing (adj.) **1:** lying under or below *(the desert and the underlying oil
deposit)* **2:** ROOT; BASIC *(underlying cause)*

Health
Anxiety

Vocabulary: surge   muddle through   swell

Mini-Lesson: Drawing Conclusions

Literacy Practice: Magazine Article

"TRY NOT TO MAKE THE DOCTOR NERVOUS -- THIS WILL BE HIS FIRST OPERATION."

▶▶ Discussion

Some people feel nervous, or anxious, in social situations. For example, one friend may feel nervous meeting new people at a party. Another may feel anxious asking for help to find an item in a grocery store.

What other social situations cause some people to feel anxious? Write your ideas here.

_____

_____

_____

_____

Read the following passage to find out what social situations can cause anxiety.

Anxiety

The supervisor pinned up the week's schedule. He turned around, eyeing the employees seated in the lunch area. "If there's a problem with the shift changes," he said, "speak now or forever hold your peace."

Kim's heart began to race. She was scheduled to work Tuesday night—the night her teacher was giving a review for the GED exams. Kim needed to ask for a shift change, but she could barely breathe. "What if he says 'no' in front of everyone?" thought Kim. "Everyone will stare at me. I'll make a fool of myself."

Kim's supervisor left the lunch area. The moment for speaking up had passed. Kim almost felt relieved.

© www.iStockphoto.com/ifotoksa

Stop and Think:

Imagine you are Kim. Why do you _almost_ feel relieved?

Many people feel a bit nervous when speaking in front of others. Their palms turn clammy, stomachs tighten, and hearts beat faster. Feeling a little nervous is beneficial; it makes one more alert and focused. But, for some people, like Kim, speaking in front of others goes far beyond feeling nervous. Speaking in front of others triggers intense anxiety.

When a person feels overwhelmed by anxiety, their heart can pound up to an alarming 150 beats per minute. This **surge** of adrenalin causes a person to sweat or feel nauseated and light-headed. For some, just the thought of voicing an opinion or being called on in class leads to blushing, trembling, and even stomach upset. For others, taking tests or exams triggers similar symptoms of anxiety.

> The average heart rate for adults is 70 to 90 beats per minute.

> **adrenalin:** hormone that the body produces because of excitement, fear, or anger

For most people, pre-exam jitters are common. But taking a test leads to distress for people who suffer from anxiety. They **muddle through** the test, struggling to focus and organize their thoughts. Their minds go blank as the facts studied the night before are lost in growing panic and confusion. As feelings of anxiety **swell**, their levels of performance drop.

Stop and Think:

How do you feel when taking a test?
Why do you feel this way?

Speaking up and taking tests are not the only triggers of anxiety. Everyday social situations such as making a phone call, entering a room full of people, or eating in public can also cause intense anxiety. The fear of being judged or watched causes some people to avoid being around people at all costs. And the costs can be high—avoiding meetings at work or missing school events.

Seeing a loved one fall victim to anxiety is painful. Providing support can help the loved one develop coping skills. Imagine a friend who feels anxious about making a phone call to see a doctor. You can support your friend by inviting her to talk about her feelings. Or you can role-play the phone call with her.

role-play:
act the part
of a person
or character,
often to model
behaviour

Stop and Think:

Why do you think the author suggests role-playing the phone call, but not making the phone call for your friend?

Feelings of anxiety may never completely disappear. But with support, patience, and understanding many people can deal with their anxiety. They can learn to face social situations that once left them feeling breathless, frustrated, and silenced.

Check the ideas you wrote on page 51 about anxiety.
Can you find your ideas in the passage?
If not, do your ideas connect in some way
to the ideas in the passage? How?

▶▶ **Discussion**

1. Think about a family member or friend who suffers (or has suffered) from anxiety. What causes their anxiety? How does their anxiety affect their life?

2. What are the three *main* causes of anxiety described in the passage?

3. In your own words, explain how intense anxiety affects a person who is taking a test.

4. A friend's social life is limited because meeting new people triggers her anxiety. The three strategies listed below are ways you could support your friend. In your opinion, which strategy is the best one?

   (a) Spend a lot of time with your friend so she is not lonely.

   (b) Make your friend meet new people by bringing her to parties and pubs.

   (c) Introduce your friend to your close friends one-by-one.

5. Why do you think speaking in front of others makes some people anxious? What strategies can people use to reduce anxiety, or nervousness, when they need to speak up?

Summarizing

Reread paragraphs 4 and 5 of the passage, on page 52.
Choose the best summary.

   (a) Intense anxiety can lead to severe physical reactions. The heart beats faster. People suffer from stomach upset.

   (b) When people feel nervous, they experience symptoms such as clammy hands and tight stomachs.

   (c) Most people feel some anxiety when speaking in public. Feeling intense anxiety can lead to severe physical reactions.

Explain your choice.
   Does the summary you chose
      • **contain the most important idea from each paragraph?**
      • **omit details such as quotes, examples, and descriptions?**

Vocabulary

Circle the best meaning for each bolded word.
Figure out what the word means by looking at how it is used in the sentence.

1. The 2010 Olympics were held in Vancouver, British Columbia. This created a **surge** of interest in the Olympics among Canadians.
   (a) lack; not enough of something
   (b) disappearance
   (c) hidden feeling
   (d) sudden, huge increase

2. I **muddled through** my income tax forms as best I could. I had no idea what I was doing. It took me two days to finish all the forms.
   (a) ripped up into small pieces
   (b) did without skill or efficiency
   (c) did quickly without much thought
   (d) completed with satisfaction

3. A movie's background music often **swells** during emotional moments. I usually turn the volume down.
   (a) moves quickly
   (b) entertains; makes someone laugh
   (c) increases more than normal
   (d) softens

Write an answer for each question. Use complete sentences.

1. A **surge** of electricity is created when lightning hits a power line. A power surge can blow fuses or damage appliances in your home. What can you do to prevent power surges during a lightning storm?

   _____

   _____

2. We sometimes **muddle through** new tasks such as setting up voice mail on a cell phone. Describe the last time you muddled through an unfamiliar task. What helped you complete the task?

   _____

   _____

3. What two things would make the population of a city **swell**?

   _____

   _____

Mini-Lesson: Drawing Conclusions

A conclusion is a decision based on two or more facts. We draw conclusions by combining or comparing facts.

Read the following three facts about feeling nervous.
Circle the correct conclusion below.

Feeling a little nervous is beneficial.

Pre-exam jitters are common.

Many people feel a bit nervous when speaking in front of others.

(a) People should avoid writing exams and speaking in front of others.

(b) A lot of people feel nervous at one time or another.

Did you choose (b)? If yes, you are right. Two of the facts suggest that feeling nervous is a common experience.

Review the bar graph on the following page. Use the bar graph to fill in the percentage for each fact below. Then choose the correct conclusion for each set of facts.

Facts

1. (a) _____ percent of people experience insomnia because of mental strain.

   (b) _____ percent of people experience a change in eating habits.

   (c) _____ percent of people have trouble digesting.

Conclusion: (a) Mental strain affects sleeping and eating habits.

(b) Poor diet leads to mental health problems.

Facts

2. (a) _____ percent of people experience headaches.

   (b) _____ percent of people experience neck or back pain.

   (c) _____ percent of people experience joint or muscular pain.

Conclusion: (a) People under mental strain should take aspirin.

               (b) Mental strain sometimes leads to physical pain.

Facts

3. (a) _____ percent of people feel fatigued because of mental strain.

   (b) _____ percent of people have insomnia.

   (c) _____ percent of people get sick more often.

Conclusion: (a) Few people get ill from mental strain.

               (b) Many people under mental strain get sick or tired.

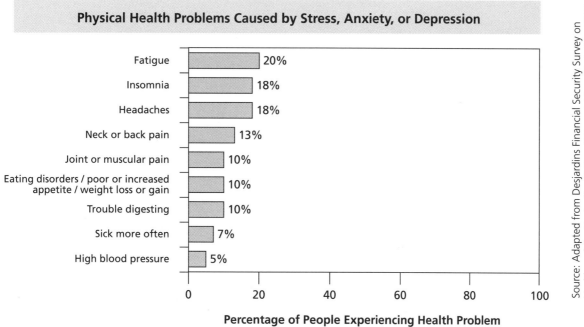

Physical Health Problems Caused by Stress, Anxiety, or Depression

Percentage of People Experiencing Health Problem

- Fatigue: 20%
- Insomnia: 18%
- Headaches: 18%
- Neck or back pain: 13%
- Joint or muscular pain: 10%
- Eating disorders / poor or increased appetite / weight loss or gain: 10%
- Trouble digesting: 10%
- Sick more often: 7%
- High blood pressure: 5%

Source: Adapted from Desjardins Financial Security Survey on Health and the Desjardins National Financial Security Index, 2006. Total number of people surveyed: 200.

How does stress affect you?
Compare how stress affects you with the facts presented in the bar graph.

Literacy Practice: Magazine Article

People read magazines for different reasons—for personal interest, to get the news, or for entertainment. Readers often do not read a magazine from beginning to end. Readers pick and choose what they want to read.

Active readers preview a magazine article, and **then decide if they want to read the rest of the article.** Previewing means getting an idea of the article's content. Previewing includes looking at pictures, the headline, the strapline, callouts, and headings.

Previewing an article also includes reading the first paragraph. The first paragraph of a magazine article tries to grab the reader's attention. It might describe an interesting event. Or it might mention interesting details that are discussed more fully in other parts of the article.

Preview the magazine article on the following page.
After you preview, mark the following sentences true (T) or false (F).

1. Girls are good for a family. _____

2. Girls benefit your health. _____

3. About 500 girls answered the survey. _____

4. It is better to have a brother than a sister. _____

5. Siblings are brothers and sisters. _____

▶▶ Discussion

How do you feel about the article after previewing it?
    Do you want to read the rest of the article?
    How did previewing help you decide?

Headline

Siblings of Sisters are Happier, More Optimistic

Strapline

Study Shows that Girls Aid Family Communication and Improve Health

By Victoria Anisman-Reiner

Which is better—sisters or brothers? Science has actually found the answer. A survey of nearly 600 young adults shows that people with sisters have a more positive outlook. They talk more with their families. And people with sisters have fewer mental health problems.

Heading

Sisters, Brothers, and Your Lifelong Outlook on Happiness

A recent study shows that growing up with at least one girl in the family helps people to communicate better. Communicating better leads to greater happiness and optimism. "Sisters appear to encourage more open communication and cohesion in families," said the study's lead researcher. And expressing emotions is basic to good mental health.

The study included 571 people between the ages of 17 and 25. They answered questions about their families, outlook on life, and mental health.

The study found that brothers have the opposite effect on their siblings' mental health and happiness. This is probably because they talk less about their

© BigStockPhoto/Artistic Captures Photography

Callout

Having a sister makes you happier, more optimistic, more balanced and probably healthier in the long run.

emotions. The study also found that girls with sisters are independent and want to achieve more.

Boys who only had brothers had the lowest scores on the survey.

One researcher says, "With boys... it is about a conspiracy of silence... Girls tend to break that down. We may have to think carefully about the way we deal with families with lots of boys."

Adapted with permission of the author.

Dictionary Use

Mark the following statements true (T) or false (F).
Use the dictionary entries as needed.

1. You can **distress** a table with a hammer or chisel. _____

2. A **pound** is less than 12 ounces. _____

3. It is possible to pay for food with **pounds**. _____

4. A ballerina usually **pounds** across the stage. _____

5. A woman would look odd if she wore a **shift**. _____

---

dis-tress (n.) **1:** extreme trouble, anxiety, sadness, etc. **2:** a difficult situation due to not having enough money, food, etc. *(She helps people in distress.)*

dis-tress (v.) **1:** to worry or upset *(The news distressed him.)* **2:** to scratch or mark something in order to make it look old or used

pound (n.) **1:** a unit of weight equal to 16 ounces **2:** a basic unit of money used in Britain and other countries **3:** a place where stray or homeless animals are kept **4:** the name for the symbol (#)

pound (v.) **1:** to hit something with force again and again **2:** to work hard at something for a long time *(pound away at homework)* **3:** to move with heavy, loud steps *(He pounded down the hall in anger.)*

shift (n.) **1:** a change in position or direction **2:** a time period of work, often eight hours **3:** a group of people who work together for a specific period of time *(the night shift)* **4:** a loose fitting, straight dress

shift (v.) **1:** to change position or move *(The wind shifted.)* **2:** to change to a different opinion, belief, etc. *(Public opinion shifted.)* **3:** to change gears while driving **4:** to move something from one place to another *(shift the blame to someone else)*

Environment
Tree Planting

© iStockphoto/Claudiad

Vocabulary: empower   blockade   depleted

Mini-Lesson: Problem-Solution

Literacy Practice: Bar Graph

© www.CartoonStock.com/Ronaldo Dias

Birds protect a tree from a lumberjack.

▶▶ Discussion

"You can make a difference."

How do you feel when you hear this statement?

      Inspired? Doubtful? Frustrated?

Why do you feel this way?

Wangari Maathai is an activist from Kenya. She fights to protect the environment. Wangari made a difference in her country. What do you think it was? Write your ideas here.

_____

_____

_____

Read the following passage to find out how Wangari made a difference in her country.

Tree Planting

Imagine planting 40 million trees. Sound impossible? To everyone in Kenya it did—except Wangari Maathai.

Wangari Maathai was born in rural Kenya in 1940. From a young age, Wangari felt that people's identities were shaped by nature—by what they saw, smelled, and touched. Her older brother recognized Wangari's love of nature and helped her leave Africa to study biology in the US.

Dry riverbed in Kenya.

When Wangari returned to Kenya, she was asked to research a disease that was infecting cattle. This research took Wangari into poor rural areas. Wangari was shocked to see that the earth was naked.

Stop and Think:

What do you think Wangari saw? Read on to see if your ideas match the passage.

The trees had been cut down for firewood. Rain carried away topsoil. Silt clogged the rivers and streams that gave life to rural communities. The clean waterways and wooded hillsides of Wangari's youth had disappeared.

Many women voiced concerns over the lack of firewood. Wangari began to see a link between the environment and poverty. Without trees, fertile soil washed away and rivers ran dry. Without firewood, rural women could not cook enough food to keep their families healthy. Without food and water, people became hungry and sick.

In 1977, Wangari formed the Green Belt Movement, an organization that paid poor women to plant trees. The movement started with one small group of women planting trees. Over the next 30 years, thousands of women's groups across Africa planted over 40 million trees. Planting trees

Wangari Maathai
(wun-GAR-ee ma-TIE)

Up to 90 percent of rural Africans use firewood as a source of energy for cooking and heating.

Women were paid about 4¢ for every tree they planted that lived.

ENVIRONMENT

reduced soil erosion, restored woodlands, and cleaned up the waterways.

Perhaps more important, the simple act of planting a tree **empowered** women in Africa. The women became the keepers of the environment. The Green Belt Movement became a tool that helped women stand up for their rights and the rights of their communities.

Planting trees alone was not enough to fight poverty and deforestation. Kenya's corrupt government allowed forested land to be clear-cut in order to grow cash crops like tea and coffee. Wangari fought the government. She led protest marches and **blockaded** forests. Wangari knew the protesters had to avoid breaking the law. She advised the women "to move wisely like the serpent but with the gentleness of the dove." Still, the women protesters were beaten, jailed, and threatened. But in the end, they forced political change.

> **cash crops:** grown to make money. Cash crops take up land that could be used to grow basic food such as rice.

> **serpent:** snake

Stop and Think:

Imagine you are one of the women protesters. What keeps you fighting against the government?

Wangari showed the world how environment, poverty, and peace go hand in hand. "Resources become **depleted**," she said, "water becomes finished, wells dry up, and the next thing you hear is that tribesmen are fighting a war." In 2004, Wangari received the Nobel Peace Prize, the first ever given to a black woman. And the first ever given to an environmental activist.

Wangari's work continues. Wangari describes herself as the hummingbird that tries to put out a forest fire. When other animals make fun of her, the hummingbird says, "I'm doing what I can."

• • • • • • • • • • • • • • • • •

Check the ideas you wrote on page 61 about Wangari.
Can you find your ideas in the passage?
> If not, do your ideas connect in some way to the ideas in the passage? How?

▶▶ Discussion

1. "Wangari felt that people's identities were shaped by nature—by what they saw, smelled, and touched." What has shaped your identity?

2. Describe how the Green Belt Movement improved (a) the environment and (b) people's lives.

3. In your own words, explain the links that Wangari makes between (a) the environment and health, and (b) health and poverty.

4. Explain Wangari's comparison between herself and a hummingbird.

5. Who do you know that made a difference in someone's life, their community, or their country? Describe the difference they made and how they went about making the change.

Summarizing

Reread paragraphs 7 and 8 of the passage, on page 63.
Choose the best summary.

(a) Kenya's government was corrupt. They allowed forests to be clear-cut.

(b) Wangari started the Green Belt Movement. She advised women "to move wisely like the serpent but with the gentleness of the dove."

(c) The Green Belt Movement empowered women. Wangari helped women protest Kenya's corrupt government and force political change.

Explain your choice.
   Does the summary you chose
   • contain the most important idea from each paragraph?
   • omit details such as quotes, examples, and descriptions?

Vocabulary

Circle the best meaning for each bolded word.
Figure out what the word means by looking at how it is used in the sentence.

1. The union **empowered** the workers. At long last, the workers were able to strike for better pay and conditions.
   (a) discouraged by making fun of   (b) provided a voice to make change
   (c) took power away from   (d) entertained in order to distract

2. Thousands of cyclists **blockaded** the main bridge downtown. Traffic during rush hour was backed up across the city.
   (a) opened up   (b) prevented entry onto
   (c) built   (d) removed completely

3. The salmon population is **depleted**. A hundred years ago, you could catch salmon with your bare hands as they swam by in the thousands.
   (a) full of life   (b) fast-moving
   (c) jumping up and down   (d) having little or nothing left

Write an answer for each question. Use complete sentences.

1. Working together for a common cause **empowers** people to create change. For example, some people start a petition. In what other ways can people work together to take control of their lives and create change?

_____

_____

2. Environmental groups sometimes **blockade** forests to prevent logging companies from clear-cutting the land. Do you think environmental groups should interfere with the logging industry? Why or why not?

_____

_____

3. Some experts say that our supply of fresh water is becoming **depleted**. What might cause the depletion of our fresh water supply?

_____

_____

Mini-Lesson: Problem-Solution

Good writers show the reader how their ideas are organized. One way to organize ideas is to present a problem, provide solutions, and state results.

Look at the problem-solution idea map below.
What is the problem?

Reread paragraphs 6 and 7 of the passage *Tree Planting*.
Identify the solution for the problem. Identify the results of the solution.
Then complete the problem-solution idea map.

Problem
Soil washed away and rivers ran dry because trees were cut down.

Solution

Results

Look at the problem-solution idea map below.
What is the problem?

Reread paragraph 8 of the passage *Tree Planting*.
Identify the solution for the problem. Identify the results of the solution.
Then complete the problem-solution idea map.

Problem
Poverty and deforestation continued because Kenya's corrupt government allowed forested land to be clear-cut.

Solution

Results

Literacy Practice: Bar Graph

Graphs show a lot of information, or data, using few words. We use bar graphs to show and compare data. When reading a bar graph, we must pay attention to the title, the two axes, the bars, and the key.

Use the bar graph to answer the questions below.

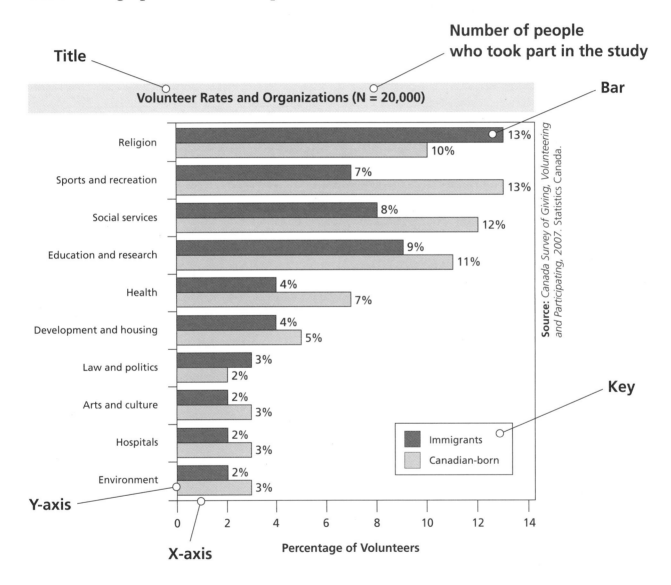

1. What is the title of the bar graph? _____

2. (a) How many people were involved in the study? _____

ENVIRONMENT

(b) What if 100,000 people were involved in the study? Would this make a difference in how much trust you put in the results of the study? Explain why or why not.

_____

3. How many different types of organizations are shown on the bar graph? _____

4. What do the numbers at the end of the bars represent? _____

5. Why are there two different shades of bars? _____

6. The **source** tells us that Statistics Canada collected the data. Why is it important to know who collected the data?

_____

7. (a) Overall, which group does more volunteer work?

   (i) immigrants   (ii) Canadian-born

   (b) Why do you think this group volunteers more than the other group?

   _____

8. (a) Which group does more legal and political volunteer work?

   (i) immigrants   (ii) Canadian-born

   (b) Why do you think this group does more legal and political work?

   _____

9. (a) Where would you place yourself on this graph? _____

   (b) What would you like to do as a volunteer in this type of organization? _____

   _____

10. Where would you place Wangari Maathai on the graph? _____

11. (a) What does this bar graph suggest about volunteers, environmental organizations, and the environment?

   _____

   (b) Give a possible reason for the situation you described in (a).

   _____

Dictionary Use

Mark the following statements true (T) or false (F).
Use the dictionary entries as needed.

1. A **clog** that does not fit well will cause pain in your arms. _____

2. **Clogs** will probably protect your feet if you walk over broken glass. _____

3. Some **identities** involve numbers. _____

4. A thief will often **restore** the things that he has stolen. _____

5. **Restoring** a house means filling it up with things you do not need anymore. _____

---

clog (n.) **1:** a shoe with a thick sole **2:** something that acts as a physical block (*a clog in the drain*)

clog (v.) **clogged; clogging** to block or become blocked (*grease clogged the pipe; traffic clogs at rush hour*)

i-den-ti-ty (n.) **identities** (pl.) **1:** who someone is (*You will need to show proof of identity.*) **2:** the qualities, beliefs, etc., that make a person or group different from others (*Children develop their own identities.*) **3:** an equation in math (*$(x + 1)^2 = x^2 + 2x + 1$*)

re-store (v.) **restored; restoring 1:** to return something, usually stolen (*restore the wallet to its owner*) **2:** to put something back into use (*The operation restored her hearing.*) **3:** to put something back to its original physical condition (*restore a building*)

Environment

Community Gardens

© PhotoLibrary

Vocabulary: staple   sporadic   hardy

Mini Lesson: Problem-Solution

Literacy Practice: Cost of a Recipe

© www.CartoonStock.com/Steve Delmonte

"I'm on the inflation diet. Every week I spend the same amount of money and come home with less food!"

▶▶ Discussion

The cost of living makes it hard to afford basics such as housing, clothing, and food. How can people cope with the high cost of living?

People in the northern community of Inuvik pay very high prices for food, especially produce. What do you think the people of Inuvik did to lower food costs? Write your ideas here.

_____

_____

_____

_____

Read the following passage to find out how the people of Inuvik lowered food costs.

Community Gardens

Bill the fruit man is a welcome sight as he rolls into Inuvik, a remote town in Canada's far north. His 16-metre (53-foot) trailer is weighed down with fresh produce and food **staples**. Shoppers line up, eager to check out the quality and prices of this month's selection. Today Bill is selling oranges at a rate of $22 a crate. Expensive? Not for residents of Inuvik. Bill's produce prices are the best in town.

Inuvik Community Greenhouse.

In remote communities north of the Arctic Circle, people grapple with the high cost of food. Food must be shipped great distances to reach northern towns, and transport costs are high. Food supplies are usually shipped in by sea or flown in by small planes. Winter ice blocks ports, and storms shut down local airports, so food deliveries are **sporadic**.

The highway that links Inuvik to southern towns is closed for up to four months of the year due to weather. As the three local grocery stores run low on supplies, food prices increase even more. Shoppers check expiry dates and pick through wilting heads of lettuce trying to get the most value for their precious food dollars.

Families across the North spend up to two-thirds of their monthly income on food.

Stop and Think:

Why do you think lettuce wilts on the grocery store shelves?

The people of Inuvik have responded to high produce prices by building the world's most northern greenhouse. Gardeners grow a wealth of produce from **hardy** veggies like broccoli and squash to sweet melons and herbs. The variety of produce expands as gardeners try growing luxury foods such as strawberries and spinach.

Stop and Think:

Why do you think strawberries and spinach are called luxury foods?

The greenhouse, built from an old hockey arena, has two floors. The top floor is used for growing bedding plants and flowers. These plants and flowers are sold to the public. The local government buys flowers to fill the hanging baskets and window boxes that add beauty to the town's public places.

The lower floor houses a community garden that boasts over 80 garden plots maintained by more than 100 gardeners. For 15 hours of volunteer work and an annual fee as low as $25, gardeners can take advantage of the benefits of indoor gardening. Inuvik's summers are cool and its soil is poor. Blackflies come out in full force during June and July. So the waiting list to get a garden plot in the greenhouse continues to grow.

Stop and Think:

Imagine you are a member of Inuvik's community greenhouse. As a volunteer, what can you offer the greenhouse?

The greenhouse doubles as a community centre. People meet to picnic and socialize in its year-round warmth. Plots are set aside for elders and community groups. Children garden side by side with parents and grandparents.

The Inuvik Community Greenhouse ensures a harvest of healthy produce in an area where fresh food is scarce and costly. One day, perhaps, Bill the fruit man will retire knowing that the residents of Inuvik can have their fill of greens every day.

The Inuvik Community Greenhouse was started by a non-profit society in 1989.

• • • • • • • • • • • • • • • •

Check the ideas you wrote on page 71 about the cost of living in Inuvik. Can you find your ideas in the passage?

If not, do your ideas connect in some way to the ideas in the passage? How?

►► Discussion

1. How do you rate fresh produce in your community in terms of cost, quality, and availability? Explain your answers.

   excellent   good   not-so-good   terrible

2. Find two reasons why food costs are high in northern Canada.

3. Find three benefits that the community greenhouse offers the residents of Inuvik.

4. There is a waiting list of people wanting to get a garden plot. Why is the top floor of the greenhouse not used for gardening plots?

5. Would your community benefit from a community garden? How? What steps would a community need to take in order to start a community garden?

Summarizing

Reread paragraphs 5 and 6 of the passage, on page 73.
Choose the best summary of these paragraphs.

(a) The top floor of the greenhouse is used to grow plants and flowers, which are sold to the public. The bottom floor has garden plots, which the residents of Inuvik use to grow produce.

(b) The government of Inuvik buys plants and flowers from the community greenhouse. The government uses these plants and flowers to beautify the town.

(c) Many residents want a plot in the community garden because it is difficult to garden outdoors in Inuvik. For instance, there are many blackflies in the summer.

Explain your choice.
   Does the summary you chose
   • contain the most important idea from each paragraph?
   • omit details such as quotes, examples, and descriptions?

Vocabulary

Circle the best meaning for each bolded word.
Figure out what the word means by looking at how it is used in the sentence.

1. Rice is a **staple** in Asian diets; potatoes are a staple for many Canadians.
   (a) main part or element   (b) healthy but rare item
   (c) dangerous choice   (d) something that is too expensive to buy

2. Her ex-husband's offers to help with the children were **sporadic**. She could not count on him to babysit when she got a full-time job.
   (a) not appreciated; annoying   (b) occurring irregularly or randomly
   (c) dependable   (d) sudden but predictable

3. **Hardy** animals usually live longer than weaker animals.
   (a) sick; having a pale colour   (b) not enough
   (c) wild   (d) strong; can survive hard conditions

Write an answer for each question. Use complete sentences.

1. Most people develop food habits. They tend to buy certain foods week after week. What food **staples** always appear on your shopping list?

   _____

   _____

2. In some areas, rainfall is predictable. For example, it always rains a lot in the spring. In other areas, rainfall is **sporadic**. How would you describe rainfall in your area— predictable or sporadic? Explain why.

   _____

   _____

3. Some jobs, such as tarring roads on a hot day, require healthy people who can work under hard conditions. What is another job requiring **hardy** workers? Explain why.

   _____

   _____

Mini-Lesson: Problem-Solution

One way to organize ideas is to present a problem, provide solutions, and state results.

Read the following paragraph.
Identify the problem, solutions, and results.

The members of the community garden were angry. Their vegetables were disappearing. The next spring, the gardeners put up a fence. But come harvest time, veggies were missing again. And it would cost the gardeners $250 to replace the broken gate in the fence. So they removed the gate. The following spring, the gardeners tried something new. They set aside a public garden plot in the community garden. And they hung a sign on the fence—"Please help yourself to the veggies in our public plot." Come harvest time, the gardeners' plots were untouched. A sign appeared in the public plot. It read: "Thank you. God bless."

Look at the problem-solution idea map below.
Fill in the missing information with the ideas from the paragraph above.

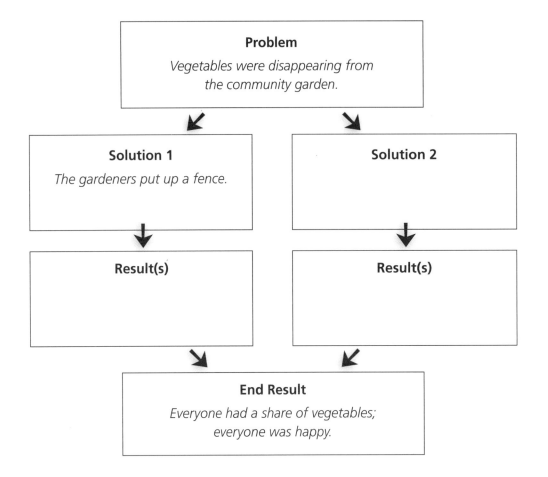

Problem
Vegetables were disappearing from the community garden.

Solution 1
The gardeners put up a fence.

Solution 2

Result(s)

Result(s)

End Result
Everyone had a share of vegetables; everyone was happy.

Reread the passage *Community Gardens.*
Finish the problem-solution idea map.

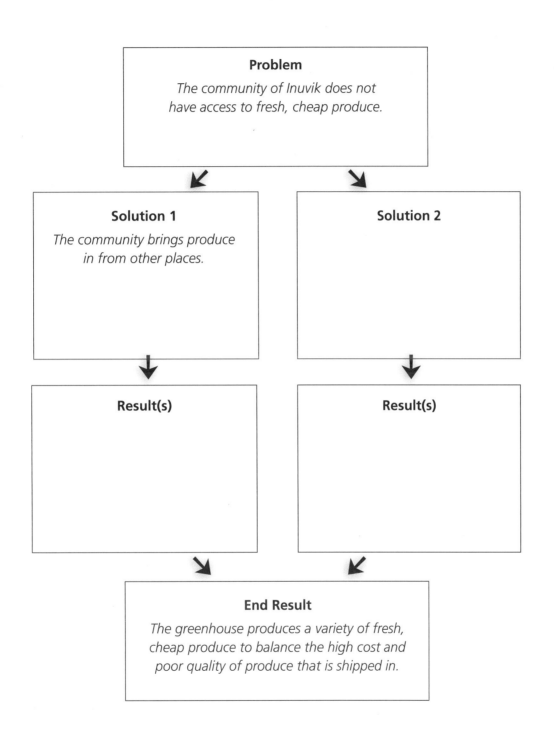

Problem

The community of Inuvik does not have access to fresh, cheap produce.

Solution 1

The community brings produce in from other places.

Solution 2

Result(s)

Result(s)

End Result

The greenhouse produces a variety of fresh, cheap produce to balance the high cost and poor quality of produce that is shipped in.

Literacy Practice: Cost of a Recipe

Everyone knows the advantages of home-cooked meals over ready-made meals. Meals cooked at home are fresher and more nutritious. Recipes can be adjusted to suit different tastes. For example, more hot spices can be added, or less salt used. Also, fresh fruit and vegetables can replace canned or frozen produce.

But with the price of fruit and vegetables these days, is home cooking cheaper than buying ready-made meals?

Use the recipe below and the listed costs to answer the questions that follow.

Recipe: Vegetable Soup (8 servings)

Ingredients

6 cups vegetable stock	½ head small cabbage
4 large tomatoes	1 ½ tablespoons Italian seasoning
1 medium potato	1 can (341 mL) corn niblets
1 medium onion	1 medium zucchini
2 stalks celery	salt and pepper to taste
2 medium carrots	

Recipe Ingredients: $13.60 (Cost does not include seasonings.)

Campbell's Vegetable Soup (1 can / 2 servings): $ .99

Knorr Vegetable Soup Mix (1 package / 4 servings): $2.45

---

1. How many servings does the vegetable soup recipe make? _____

2. (a) How many servings does one can of Campbell's soup make? _____

   (b) How many cans of soup would you need to make eight servings? _____

   (c) What would be the cost of eight servings of Campbell's soup? _____

   (d) How many servings does one package of Knorr soup make? _____

(e) How many packages of soup would you need to make eight servings? _____

(f) What would be the cost of eight servings of Knorr soup? _____

3. The cost of salt and pepper is not included in the cost of the ingredients for the homemade soup. Should it be? Explain your answer.

_____

_____

4. What is one hidden cost of making homemade soup? (HINT: Hidden costs are not obvious. Hidden costs are not always related to money.)

_____

_____

5. Would you substitute the canned corn with frozen corn? Why or why not?

_____

_____

6. Would the price of the homemade soup always be the same? Explain your answer.

_____

_____

7. Which soup would you serve your family—one of the prepared soups or the homemade soup? Give two reasons for your choice.

_____

_____

_____

And what do you think?

The cost of healthy foods varies from province to province. Even city to city. For example, a bag of brown rice is about $2.19 in Toronto, Ontario, $7.76 in Winnipeg, Manitoba, and $11.99 in Rankin Inlet, Nunavut.

Source: Edmonton Journal, *Drastic price variation of healthy foods*, Feb. 2009.

Dictionary Use

Mark the following statements true (T) or false (F).
Use the dictionary entries as needed.

1. Hitting a perfect **boast** requires a rifle. _____

2. A false **boast** is like an exaggeration. _____

3. It is against the rules for wrestlers to **grapple**. _____

4. A sailboat's **grapple** can be made of heavy metal. _____

5. Libraries offer a **wealth** of information. _____

---

boast (n.) **1:** a statement you express with too much pride *(His boast about being a good cook was proven to be a lie.)* **2:** a reason to be proud *(Our greatest boast is our son.)* **3:** a shot in the racquet game of squash

boast (v.) **1:** BRAG **2:** to have something that is impressive *(The apartment boasts a beautiful view.)*

grap-ple (n.) **1:** a wrestling hold or grip **2:** a hand-to-hand struggle **3:** a small anchor with many prongs

grap-ple (v.) **grappled; grappling 1:** to hold and fight with another person **2:** to try to solve or deal with a problem *(grapple with seasonal flooding)*

wealth (n.) **1:** the total value of what somebody or something owns **2:** a large amount

---

ENVIRONMENT

© Fumi Ezaki Collection, JCNM, 96/182.1.001
Planting a Garden, Lemon Creek, ca. 1943.

History

The Japanese Canadians in World War II

Vocabulary: bar   confiscate   compensate

Mini-Lesson: Chronological Order

Literacy Practice: Photo

© CP images, ca. 1942–1946

Japanese families being removed from their homes.

▶▶ Discussion

World War II began in 1939. On December 7, 1941, Japan bombed US ships in Pearl Harbor, Hawaii. Because of this bombing, the Canadian government punished Japanese Canadians.

What do you know about the history of Japanese Canadians? What would you like to know? Write your questions here.

1. _____

2. _____

3. _____

Read the following passage to find the answers to your questions.

The Japanese Canadians in World War II

In the late 1870s, Japanese people began to immigrate to western Canada. They came from fishing villages and farms in Japan, in the hope of building a better life in Canada. The first migrants were single men, who settled along the coast of British Columbia. The men were soon joined by young Japanese women.

© Fumi Ezaki Collection, JCNM, 96/182.1.001, Planting a Garden, Lemon Creek, ca. 1943

By the early 1940s, the BC government had passed many laws that made life hard. The Japanese paid taxes, yet they were denied the right to vote. Many second-generation Japanese were well-educated, yet they were **barred** from most professions. And Japanese employees were paid less than their white co-workers. Despite these laws, the BC coast became home to over 21,000 Japanese people.

In the early 1940s, about 75 percent of Japanese people living in BC were Canadian citizens.

Stop and Think:

Why do you think the Japanese people stayed in BC despite the harsh laws?

On December 7, 1941, the lives of Japanese Canadians began to crumble. Japan bombed US ships in Pearl Harbor, Hawaii. The bombing increased racist feelings against Japanese Canadians, causing an outbreak of panic and fear. The RCMP and the military knew that Japanese Canadians were not a threat to Canada's safety. Yet, the prime minister let the BC government punish Japanese Canadians for a crime they did not commit.

Pearl Harbor: US naval base in Hawaii

Stop and Think:

How do you think the BC government punished Japanese Canadians? Read on to see if your ideas match the passage.

On December 8, 1941, the Navy started to **confiscate** fishing boats from Japanese Canadians. The Canadian Pacific Railway fired

Japanese workers. Many other Canadian industries did the same. Japanese newspapers and schools were shut down.

A few months after Pearl Harbor was bombed, the BC government relocated over 20,000 Japanese Canadians. Family members were allowed to take two suitcases each from their homes. The government confiscated and sold Japanese homes and property, erasing the lives that Japanese Canadians had worked so hard to build.

Many young Japanese Canadian men were sent to work in road-building camps. Others were sent to work on beet farms in the prairies. Women, children, and older men were sent to relocation camps throughout BC. Families lived in cramped wooden shacks. In winter, ice built up on the thin plywood walls. Mothers had little money and struggled to buy enough food for their children.

World War II ended in 1945. The government made Japanese Canadians leave BC. Many moved to other parts of Canada. In 1946, the government tried to deport 10,000 Japanese Canadians. Public protests across Canada stopped the effort, but only after 4,000 Japanese Canadians were exiled to Japan. In 1949, Japanese Canadians were once again free to live anywhere in Canada.

Japanese Canadians worked hard to make the government admit to past mistakes. In 1988, the federal government made a public apology to Japanese Canadians. The government gave 12,000 Japanese Canadians $21,000 each. This money was meant to **compensate** for government actions during the war.

> Over 700 Japanese Canadians resisted separation from their families. They were put in prison camps called **internment camps**.

Stop and Think:

Do you think the government owed Japanese Canadians an apology for its actions? Why or why not?

The story of the Japanese Canadians reminds us not to repeat the mistakes of the past.

• • • • • • • • • • • • • • • • •

Check the questions you wrote on page 81 about Japanese Canadians. Did the information in the passage answer your questions? Did the information in the passage make you think of new questions?
    If yes, what are your new questions?

▶▶ Discussion

1. If you had to relocate in a hurry, what would you pack in your suitcase? Explain why you would pack those items.

2. Explain why the Canadian government relocated Japanese Canadians after the bombing of Pearl Harbor.

3. Describe the racism that Japanese Canadians experienced before, during, and after World War II.

4. Why do you think it took the Canadian government more than 45 years to apologize to Japanese Canadians?

5. Why do you think people immigrate to Canada? Do you think some newcomers in Canada experience discrimination? Explain your answer.

Summarizing

Reread paragraphs 1 and 2 of the passage, on page 82.
Choose the best summary.

(a) Japanese people began to immigrate to Canada in the late 1870s. By the early 1940s, over 21,000 Japanese people had settled along the coast of BC.

(b) Japanese people came to Canada looking for a better life. By the early 1940s, the BC government had passed racist laws that affected all Japanese Canadians.

(c) Japanese people came to Canada in the hope of building a better life. But they were treated unfairly. The Japanese paid taxes, yet they could not vote.

Explain your choice.
   Does the summary you chose
      • contain the most important idea from each paragraph?
      • omit details such as quotes, examples, and descriptions?

Vocabulary

Circle the best meaning for each bolded word.

Figure out what the word means by looking at how it is used in the sentence.

1. The teen was **barred** from entering the pub because he was underage.
   (a) blocked or prevented from   (b) encouraged to try
   (c) invited into   (d) at the point of

2. The student continually used her cell phone in class. The teacher **confiscated** the phone but gave it back at the end of the day.
   (a) threw away   (b) tried to use
   (c) broke or damaged   (d) took away as a punishment

3. The insurance company **compensated** us for water damage caused by the broken water main. We received a cheque for $1,050.
   (a) congratulated or praised   (b) punished or put limits on
   (c) gave something in return for a loss (d) forced to live in another place

Write an answer for each question. Use complete sentences.

1. News reporters are often **barred** from attending meetings held by political leaders. Do you think news reporters should have open access to all political meetings? Why or why not?

   _____

   _____

2. In airports, customs employees **confiscate** living plants from people crossing a border. Why do you think it is illegal to transport plants from one country into another?

   _____

   _____

3. Companies cannot always afford to give employees a raise. Some companies **compensate** their employees in different ways. For example, they allow employees to work flex hours. Describe one other way companies can compensate their employees.

   _____

   _____

Mini-Lesson: Chronological Order

Chronological order presents events in the order that they happened.

We often use chronological order in our daily lives. For example, we use chronological order when we report an accident or describe what happened in a movie. Authors often use chronological order when they write about history or people's lives.

Active readers recognize how ideas are organized. Knowing how ideas are organized helps readers to understand the ideas.

Use the timeline on the following page to answer these questions:

1. What is the first year shown on the timeline? _____

2. What is the last year shown? _____

3. What would be the next year shown on the timeline after the year 1990? _____
   How did you figure out your answer?

4. What is the total number of years shown on the timeline? _____
   How did you figure out your answer?

5. World War II started in 1939. About how many years did World War II last? _____

6. When did the Japanese bomb Pearl Harbor?   (a) a couple of years before the war
                                                (b) during the war
                                                (c) a couple of years after the war

▶▶ Discussion

7. (a) Did the end of the war mean the end of hard times for
    Japanese Canadians? Explain your answer.

    (b) Do you think racism toward Japanese Canadians disappeared
    from the 1950s to the 1980s? Explain your answer.

8. (a) About how many years did it take, after World War II ended,
    for the government to apologize to Japanese Canadians?

    (b) Do you think racism toward Japanese Canadians disappeared
    after the government apologized? Explain your answer.

The Japanese Canadians

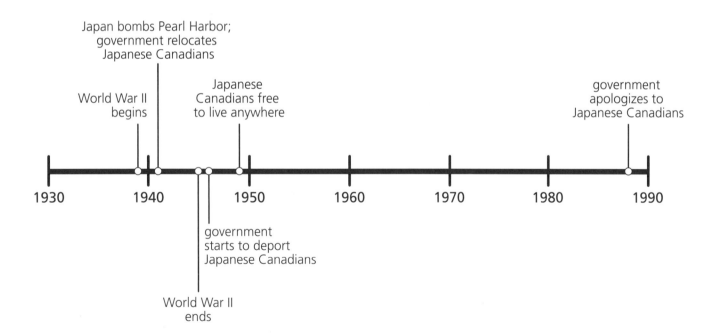

Literacy Practice: Photo

In today's world, images are often used to tell stories, send messages, and create emotions. Movies, logos, ads, graffiti, and photos are examples of communicating with images.

Reading an image means (1) looking at the details in the image (2) responding to the image, and (3) trying to figure out the story behind the image.

Analyze the two photos by discussing the following questions:

1. Describe what you see in the photo. What do you think is the most important detail in the photo? Explain why.

2. How do you feel when you look at the photo? What thoughts come to mind? What, in or about the photo, makes you respond in these ways?

3. Look at the details in the photo. What can you guess about the people's daily life? What questions come to your mind?

4. Whose story is being told in this photo? What is the story?

BC Japanese internment camp, Lemon Creek (1943).

© JCNM, Fumi Ezaki Collection, 96/182.1.002, Mrs. Take Akiyama carrying water in Lemon Creek, ca. 1943

© JCNM, Kimiko Inouye Collections, Kimiko Inouye's parlor, ca. 1943

Living room of a Japanese Canadian family (1930s).

Reread paragraphs 5 and 6 of the passage, on page 83. How do these photos affect your understanding of or response to the ideas in those two paragraphs?

And what do you think?

Japanese Canadians lost about $443 million* because of lost property and wages during World War II. They got no compensation for lost earning power after the war, or the loss of civil rights and education.

* 1986 dollars
Source: Price Waterhouse report, 1986.

Dictionary Use

Mark the following statements true (T) or false (F).
Use the dictionary entries as needed.

1. **Migrant** birds fly south for the winter. _____

2. Big farms might depend on **migrant** workers to harvest crops. _____

3. A teacup will **shatter** if you pour strong tea into it. _____

4. Winning the lottery could **shatter** a person's hopes for the future. _____

5. In golf, a hole-in-one is also called a **single**. _____

---

mi-grant (n.) **1:** a person who goes from one place to another to find work **2:** a bird or animal that moves from one area to another at different times of the year

shat-ter (v.) **1:** to break suddenly into many small pieces **2:** to damage very badly *(The end of his marriage shattered his dreams.)* **3:** to greatly upset emotionally *(She was shattered by the bad news.)*

sin-gle (n.) **1:** a person who is not married **2:** a hit in baseball that allows the hitter to get to first base **3:** a room in a hotel for one person **4:** one song from a group of songs *(a hit single from the latest CD)*

sin-gle (adj.) **1:** only one *(a single serving of dessert)* **2:** not married

---

© Glenbow Archives NA-5022-10

History
Residential Schools

Vocabulary: assimilate   compulsory   ostracize

Mini-Lesson: Chronological Order

Literacy Practice: Poem

© Canada Dept. of Mines and Technical Surveys/Library and
Archives Canada/PA-023095

Sewing class in Indian residential school
(Resolution, Northwest Territories).

▶▶ Discussion

Canada is a country of many peoples from many cultures. Over time, some groups of people begin to lose their cultural identity. Why do you think this loss occurs?

In the late 1800s, the Canadian government began to set up residential schools. These schools became a tool used to suppress the First Nations' cultural identity.

What do you know about the residential schools? What would you like to know? Write your questions here.

1. _____

2. _____

3. _____

Read the following passage to find the answers to your questions.

Residential Schools

Life in an Indian residential school was harsh. The rules were strict. Students could not practise their traditions or speak their own languages. Students who broke the rules were punished. In some residential schools, the living conditions were hard. And in others, students lacked proper food and clothing.

Old Sun School on the Blackfoot Siksika reserve (Alberta).

In the late 1800s, the Canadian government passed laws to **assimilate** Indians into Canadian society. The government passed the Indian Act in 1876. The act imposed laws that controlled all aspects of Indians' daily life.

The residential schools were a strong tool used in Canada's plan to assimilate the Indians. Churches ran the schools; the government provided the money. The schools were supposed to prepare Indians for life in white society. But the goal of the residential schools was to "kill the Indian in the child." The government hoped that native customs would disappear within a few generations.

> **Indian:** the name early white explorers gave to people in Canada. We now use the name First Nations instead of Indian.

Stop and Think:

What do you think "kill the Indian in the child" means?

By 1920, attending residential school was **compulsory** for Indian children aged 7 to 15. Priests, Indian agents, and police officers enforced attendance by taking children from their homes. The schools were often many days' journey away from the students' homes. Students lived at the schools for ten months a year. Some children returned to their homes in the summer. Others did not see their families for years.

Stop and Think:

Imagine you are a young child. You do not see your family for years. How does this separation from family affect you?

HISTORY

© Glenbow Archives NA-5022-10

By 1931, about 80 residential schools were in operation across Canada. Many of the schools were crowded and lacked proper sanitation. Students did not receive adequate health care. Because of these conditions, many students died of tuberculosis.

Most students developed some skills in reading and writing. Boys farmed or learned a trade. Girls learned to cook, sew, and wash clothes. The schools taught English or French, Christianity, and white customs. Some students liked the schools, but most students were helpless without their parents to love and protect them.

> **tuberculosis:**
> a serious disease that affects mainly the lungs; also known as TB

Stop and Think:

What do you think the quality of education was in the schools? Give a reason for your answer.

About 150,000 Aboriginal children had been removed from their communities by the time the last residential school closed in 1996. Tens of thousands of students had suffered emotional, physical, and sexual abuse. Many students who returned home found that they no longer belonged. Some were **ostracized** by their communities. Others had learned to feel ashamed of their people's way of life. At the same time, many students did not have the skills to cope in white society. They struggled to raise children and foster healthy relationships in the home. Many turned to various addictions.

Former students of the residential schools began to tell their stories. Aboriginal groups looked for ways of healing. In 1990, Aboriginal leader Phil Fontaine began to lobby the government for compensation. In 2007, the courts agreed to a compensation package of over $5 billion. In 2008, the prime minister of Canada made a public apology to First Nations peoples.

The work of healing goes on.

• • • • • • • • • • • • • • • • •

Check the questions you wrote on page 91 about residential schools.
Did the information in the passage answer your questions?
Did the information in the passage make you think of new questions?
    If yes, what are your new questions?

►► Discussion

1. Do you think today's schools prepare children for life in society? Explain your answer.

2. How did the residential schools attempt to "kill the Indian in the child"?

3. What effects did the residential schools have on Aboriginal children and families?

4. Why do you think some former students of the residential schools had difficulty raising children?

5. Do you think places of worship should be involved in educating children? Why or why not? What other roles should places of worship play or not play in our communities?

Summarizing

**Reread paragraph 7 of the passage, on page 93.
Choose the best summary.**

> (a) About 150,000 Aboriginal children attended residential schools. Some students were ostracized by their community when they returned home.

> (b) The residential schools affected the lives of Aboriginal students. Many turned to various addictions.

> (c) Aboriginal students suffered many kinds of abuse in the residential schools. These abuses had far-reaching, negative effects on their lives.

Explain your choice.
   Does the summary you chose
   • contain the most important idea from each paragraph?
   • omit details such as quotes, examples, and descriptions?

Vocabulary

Circle the best meaning for each bolded word.
Figure out what the word means by looking at how it is used in the sentence.

1. The Canadian volunteers moved to Cuba and worked in a hospital. The Cuban
   doctors tried to **assimilate** the volunteers into the Cuban way of life.
   (a) prevent people from entering   (b) make people believe in a lie
   (c) encourage people to stay the same (d) absorb people into the main culture

2. Wearing uniforms is **compulsory** in some schools. Students who do not wear their
   uniform are sent home, no questions asked.
   (a) required by law or rule   (b) forbidden by a leader
   (c) optional   (d) complicated

3. The snobby women's group **ostracized** anyone who did not come from a rich family.
   This behaviour resulted in a lack of new members joining the group.
   (a) congratulated or praised   (b) welcomed happily
   (c) refused to associate with   (d) forced to get a job

Write an answer for each question. Use complete sentences.

1. The children of newcomers usually adapt to their new society more quickly than
   their parents. Why do you think it is easier for children to **assimilate** than parents?

   _____

   _____

2. In some communities, bylaws make it **compulsory** to keep dogs tied up and cats
   on leashes. Do you agree with these bylaws? Why or why not?

   _____

   _____

3. Why do you think people with a criminal record are **ostracized** by some members
   of society?

   _____

   _____

Mini-Lesson: Chronological Order

Chronological order presents events in the order that they happened. Authors often use chronological order when they write about history or describe people's lives.

In order to show chronological order, authors use special phrases. These phrases are called time markers. These markers include phrases such as these:

in the 1990s	on January 1, 2011
at the end of the year	for three months
two months later	by the early 1940s

**Read the following paragraph. It contains seven time markers.
Underline the time markers as you read.
Then answer the questions below.**

> Phil Fontaine was born in September 1944. Six years later, his father died. And Phil found himself in a residential school, where he stayed for the next 10 years. By the early 1970s, Phil had entered politics. In 1997, he became National Chief of the Assembly of First Nations. Ten years later, Phil fought to establish a fair process for First Nations' land claims. In the same year, the courts agreed to compensate the victims of the residential school tragedy.

1. How old was Phil when he left residential school? _____

2. About how old was Phil when he entered politics? _____

3. In what year did Phil fight for land claims? _____

Now look at the timeline on the following page. It shows some important events in the history of residential schools.

**Reread the passage *Residential Schools*.
Complete the timeline by adding seven more events.**

The History of Residential Schools

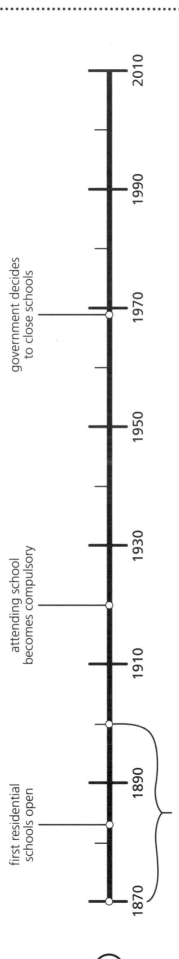

- 1870
- first residential schools open
- 1890
- attending school becomes compulsory
- 1910
- 1930
- 1950
- government decides to close schools
- 1970
- 1990
- 2010

Literacy Practice: Poem

Even when poetry has a meaning, as it usually has, it may
be inadvisable to draw it out. Perfect understanding will
sometimes almost extinguish pleasure.

—A.E. Housman (poet, 1859–1936)

What do you think Housman is saying about reading and
understanding poetry?

We sometimes feel that reading poetry is difficult because we cannot
always understand all the ideas. But reading poetry is not like reading
a recipe, a set of instructions, or a passage in a textbook. Reading
poetry can be about identifying with the author's words, emotions,
and message. As Housman suggests, we do not have to understand
a poem completely to enjoy it.

**Read the poem on the following page.
As you read, think about**

1. who the author is, and

2. why she wrote the poem.

   Circle the words and phrases in the poem that make you think
   of silence.

Read the poem again. As you read, think about

3. whose voices you hear in the poem, and

4. what the voices are saying, and why.

Read the poem a final time. As you read, underline any lines

5. that raise questions in your mind, and

6. that you can identify with or
   make a personal connection with.

   Discuss which lines you underlined and why.

Let Me Hear My Voice
by Janet Dick

My voice has been silent for too long
In the residential school.
Quiet! Hush! Don't speak!
They are the words
That I grew up hearing.

As a child
Because of cultural traditions
The family spoke for you
Or a speaker was hired
To voice family concerns.

Happy! Sad!
Still and quiet
I must remain.
Do not shame the family.
Do it our way!
Be still! Be quiet! Learn!
Don't ask questions,
Watch and learn.

No voice! No sound!
So silently, I voice my concerns
My sorrows—my prayers.

Do not shame the family
But, it is in Heaven I will speak.
Let me hear my voice!
Silence has been too long!

Reprinted with permission of The John Howard Society
of Canada and Lee Weinstein.

Dictionary Use

Mark the following statements true (T) or false (F).
Use the dictionary entries as needed.

1. A chef uses a **former** to measure liquids. _____

2. She has a **former** husband, which means she is divorced. _____

3. **Imposing** on a friend will improve the friendship. _____

4. A small **operation** might consist of an owner and one employee. _____

5. An example of an **operation** is 4 - 2 = 2. _____

---

for-mer (n.) **1:** the first of two things that have been mentioned (*If offered a choice between living in the city or the country, I'd choose the former.*) **2:** an electrical term used for a frame on which to wind wire

for-mer (adj.) **1:** happening or existing in an earlier period of time (*a shadow of her former self*) **2:** EX (*former roommate*)

im-pose (v.) **imposed; imposing** **1:** to cause something to affect someone by using your authority **2:** to take advantage of (*impose on a neighbour's kindness*)

op-er-a-tion (n.) **1:** SURGERY **2:** a business or organization **3:** a state of being used—used with *in* (*The machine is in operation.*) **4:** the way something works (*the quiet operation of the air conditioner*) **5:** a mathematical process such as addition

---

ANSWER KEY

In some cases, the answer key contains only a few of the possible responses. There are other acceptable responses for these questions.

People

Unit 1. Jane Goodall

Discussion: 1. Student responses will vary. **2.** Jane knew as a child that she wanted to study and write about animals. She left a comfortable life to go to Africa to study animals. Studying chimps in the wilds was hard, but Jane never gave up. Jane gave the chimps names and recognized their emotions. She started Roots & Shoots. She has spent her life fighting for animal rights. **3.** Scientists did not take Jane seriously at first. Then they began to see animals as she did. Jane helped a group of teens work with local villagers. She set up Roots & Shoots, which is now a worldwide organization that involves tens of thousands of young adults. **4.** Yes. Jane was the first field researcher to name animals that were being studied. Jane discovered that chimps use tools, which showed they were like humans. She set up an organization that aimed at getting young adults involved in environmental issues. **5.** Student responses will vary.

Summary: Summary (c) is the best summary. It contains the most important idea from the paragraph—Jane suffered a lot, but she made an important discovery. Summary (a) does not mention that chimps are like humans. It contains an example. Summary (b) does not contain the most important idea.

Vocabulary: 1. b **2.** d **3.** a

Mini-Lesson: (p. 6) Possible responses: **1.** The coffee was hot. (People will spit out hot coffee so they don't burn their mouth.) The milk in the coffee was sour. (People will spit out sour milk because it tastes bad.) **2.** The man is late. (People run when they are late.) The man is using a cell phone. (Lots of people talk on their cell in public places.) The man is talking to his partner. (People say "I love you" to their partners.) **(p. 7)** Possible responses: **1.** Jane was brave. (She was ready to go to Africa at a very young age. She was a woman. She had no formal training.) Jane was serious about studying animals. (She was ready to leave the comfort of her home.) **2.** Jane loved her job. Jane would have done anything to study chimpanzees. (She was willing to suffer for it.) **3.** Jane let people know it was okay to have feelings for animals. (Naming the animals showed Jane saw them as humans.) Jane set a good example for field researchers. (Researchers started to name animals, like Jane.) Researchers learned to respect Jane. (Researchers followed her example of naming animals.)

Literacy Practice: 1. Roots & Shoots **2a.** about us **2b.** find a group **2c.** Kids & Teens, Parents **3a.** Roots & Shoots finds Green Heroes **3b.** No Name Calling Week **3c.** view all events **4.** visit our store (in Roots & Shoots Store); store or cart icon (in tool bar) **5.** 3—email, phone, write

Dictionary: 1. F **2.** T **3.** T **4.** F **5.** F

Unit 2. Dalai Lama

Discussion: 1. Student responses will vary. **2.** The monks searched four years to find the Dalai Lama. The Dalai Lama and his family lived in a palace. The people refused to let the Dalai Lama give himself up to the Chinese. The people look to the Dalai Lama for hope and spiritual guidance. **3.** He began a rigorous education at the young age of six. He studied mature subjects at a young age. He became a Buddhist scholar at a young age. He dealt with the Chinese invasion when he was just a young man. **4.** a, b, and f—All of these methods are peaceful and within the law. **5.** Student responses will vary.

Summary: Summary (a) is the best summary. It contains the most important ideas from both paragraphs—the monks find the young boy and prove he is the Dalai Lama. Summary (b) contains descriptive details and does not mention that the monks find the Dalai Lama. Summary (c) does not mention that the monks prove the boy is the Dalai Lama.

Vocabulary: 1. d **2.** c **3.** c

Mini-Lesson: (p. 16) Possible responses: **1.** China is much more powerful than Tibet. The Chinese government wanted to take away the Tibetan people's way of life. China wanted complete control over Tibet. **2.** The Dalai Lama would give his life for his people. The Dalai Lama loved his people. The Dalai Lama was brave. **3.** China still controls Tibet. It is still too dangerous for the Dalai Lama to go to Tibet.
(p. 17) 1. The car would not have survived a long winter drive. **2.** I sold my car so I could fly us home. Buying Christmas gifts was out of the question that year. **3.** I went through my mom's closet and found, buried against the back wall, two of my old Barbies. **4.** My son was so young I figured he wouldn't know the difference. My children were young at the time—four years old and the other only a year and a half.
5. My mom and I were huddled under a blanket drinking hot tea and watching TV. **6.** I just cried. I always make sure that we do something to make Christmas special for at least one family that could use a little cheer.

Literacy Practice: 1. China (2010) **2.** which part of the world is shown on the main map; the location of China (and other countries shown on the map) in the world **3a.** solid, straight line **3b.** India, Nepal, Bhutan, Mongolia **4a.** broken line **4b.** iii **5.** New Delhi **6.** d **7a.** (iii) **7b.** (iii)

Dictionary: 1. F **2.** F **3.** T **4.** F **5.** T

Relationships

Unit 3. Bullying

Discussion: 1. Student responses will vary. **2.** They fear adults cannot protect them. They fear adults will not take them seriously. If bullied children speak out, bullies retaliate. Some bullied children believe they deserve to be picked on. Bullied children do not have the confidence to report bullies. **3a.** school authorities; parents; youth and community centres **3b.** School authorities can help by providing more supervision and talking with the parents of bullies. Parents can help by letting the child know bullying is not acceptable, teaching the child to use self-talk, and helping the child develop social skills and self-confidence. Youth and community centres can suggest anti-bullying strategies. **4.** Possible responses: **a.** Bullied children live a life of fear and insecurity. They may end up dropping out of school or killing themselves. **b.** Bullies become more confident because they can bully without fear of being caught or punished. Their bullying behaviour may become worse. They settle into a pattern of bullying that lasts a lifetime. **c.** Parents may not know what is going on and blame their bullied child for things that are not his/her fault, such as failing school or always pretending to be sick. Parents will worry about what is going on with their child. They may feel guilty when they realize their child was being bullied and they did nothing. **5.** Student responses will vary.

Summary: Summary (b) is the best summary. It includes the most important ideas from both paragraphs—parents can detect bullying and parents can work with educators. Summary (a) includes the idea of parents detecting bullying, but it also includes an example. Summary (c) mentions that bullied children stay silent. This idea is not developed in the paragraphs.

Vocabulary: 1. d **2.** b **3.** b

Mini-Lesson: (p. 26) Supporting Details: any 3 details listed in the paragraph **(p. 27) Paragraph 1: Main Idea:** Parents of bullied children can turn to school authorities for help. **Supporting Details:** Teachers can provide more supervision. Principals can talk to bullies' parents. Parents can get involved in anti-bullying programs. **Paragraph 2: Main Idea:** Parents can help a bullied child in different ways. **Supporting Details:** Talk to the child about difference and diversity. Teach the child how to use self-talk. Help the child develop skills for making friends. Help the child develop self-confidence.

Literacy Practice: Student responses will vary.

Dictionary: 1. F **2.** F **3.** T **4.** F **5.** T

Unit 4. Women in Gangs

Discussion: 1. Student responses will vary. **2.** They hope to make money. They need protection. They want to escape a life of abuse. They are promised a lavish lifestyle **3.** No. Male gang members force female members into a life of crime (prostitution, property theft, shoplifting). They put female members' lives at risk by using them as mules or spies in other gangs. **4.** Possible responses: Women are not respected in male gangs. Women feel safer and more powerful in all-women gangs. Women feel they have more control over their lives in all women gangs. **5.** Student responses will vary.

Summary: Summary (c) is the best summary. It contains the most important ideas from both paragraphs—women are used as drug mules and women use sex to get information for their gangs. Summary (a) includes only an example of how women are used as drug mules. Summary (b) does not mention drug mules, only smuggling cocaine. It contains only an example of how female members get information for their gangs.

Vocabulary: 1. b **2.** a **3.** c

Mini-Lesson: (p. 36) Supporting Details: Sandi got $5,000 for smuggling cocaine. By working for the gang, Sandi was able to move into a safer community. **(p. 37) Paragraph 1: Main Idea:** b **Supporting Details:** Female gangsters seduce rival gang members to find out about drug deals or where key gang members are. They seduce witnesses to gang crimes to find out how much the witnesses know.
Paragraph 2: Main Idea: c **Supporting Details:** OGs are most powerful and act as mentors to other gang members. Lookouts watch out for police. Flunkies do the dirty work of gangs.

Literacy Practice: 1. non-permanent gang activity **2.** strong gang activity **3.** The bigger black circles show that there are more gangs and gang members in that area. **4.** Possible response: The location of strong gang activity might still be accurate because these gangs stay in an area if they are thriving. The location of non-permanent gang activity may have changed by now because these gangs come and go. **5a.** iii **5b.** Possible responses: The population is bigger here than in other parts of Canada. There are a lot of big cities in this part of Canada. This part of Canada borders the United States, so gangs might be bigger because they have members from both countries. This area is on water, so gangs can smuggle drugs by boat. This area is very multi-cultural, so gangs from other countries might set up operation here. **5c.** Alberta. Possible responses: The population in the area is not big enough to support a gang. Big gangs drive smaller gangs out of an area. The population is not stable; people move around a lot. Policing might be stronger. **5d.** Possible responses: The towns are too small to support gangs. Gangs are made up of young adults, and young adults from northern towns often move south. People have more community support in small towns, so they do not need to look to gangs for protection or money. People in the north are more or less equal in terms of what they have, so they are not envious of each other; there might be more gang activity where some people feel shut out of the money. **6.** Student responses will vary.

Dictionary: 1. T **2.** F **3.** T **4.** F **5.** T

Health

Unit 5. Insomnia

Discussion: 1. Student responses will vary. **2.** They rely on caffeine, take naps, or self-medicate with alcohol and drugs. **3a.** Temporary insomnia lasts from a single night to a few weeks; chronic insomnia can last for months or years. **3b.** Temporary insomnia can be caused by daily stress; chronic insomnia can be caused by long-term stress, physical and mental conditions, and sleeping disorders. **4.** Possible responses: They do not think their sleeping problem is serious enough to see a doctor. They are afraid of doctors. They are too tired to make the effort to see a doctor. They may think a doctor will just prescribe sleeping pills. Self-medicating seems more convenient than seeing a doctor. They may think self-medicating is more effective. Self-medicating seems to be an easier solution than making lifestyle changes or going to counselling. **5.** Possible responses: having a regular evening routine, getting regular exercise, avoiding napping, balancing your diet, avoiding TV, exercise, or eating before going to bed.

Summary: Summary (a) is the best summary. It contains only the most important ideas from both paragraphs—chronic insomnia affects a person's daily life, and seeing a health care provider is better than self-medicating. Summary (b) includes the ideas of self-medicating and seeing a health care provider, but it does not say that seeing a health care provider is the better choice. Also, the summary contains only an example of how insomnia affects quality of life. Summary (c) includes the idea that insomnia affects quality of life, but it contains an example of how people self-medicate.

Vocabulary: 1. d **2.** c **3.** d

Mini-Lesson: 1a. 46 **1b.** 18 **1c.** 3 **Conclusion:** b **2a.** 16 **2b.** 18 **2c.** 12 **Conclusion:** a **3a.** 29 **3b.** 28 **3c.** 12 **Conclusion:** b

Literacy Practice: (p. 48) 1. c **2.** a **3.** f **4.** d **5.** e **6.** b, d **7.** b **(p. 49) 1.** Not until 6:00 a.m. the next morning. You cannot exceed more than four doses in 24 hours. **2.** No. You should be concerned if the fever lasts more than three days. **3a.** Don't know. The label does not mention food. **3b.** Phone 1-888-788-8181. **4a**. Possible responses: Is this safe for children? What is the dosage? How do I use it? What are the side effects? **4b.** Possible responses: Is your father on any medications? Does your father have any health issues? How old is your father? Does he have any allergies?

Dictionary: 1. F **2.** F **3.** T **4.** T **5.** T

Unit 6. Anxiety

Discussion: 1. Student responses will vary. **2.** speaking up in front of people, taking exams and tests, the fear of being watched or judged in everyday social situations (making a phone call, entering a room full of people, eating in public) **3.** The test-taker becomes more and more anxious during the exam. It becomes harder to focus. He gets confused and cannot organize ideas. He forgets what he studied and can't answer the questions. He starts to panic. His heart beats fast. He may start to shake or feel sick. **4.** (c) is most beneficial. The friend is being supported to deal with her anxiety but is not being overprotected or forced into an overwhelming social situation. **5.** Possible responses: **reasons for anxiety:** lack of self-confidence, remembering a fearful or embarrassing experience early in life, learning "anxiety behaviour" from another person, inherited personality traits **strategies:** self-talk, calm breathing, rehearsing what you want to say, having a confident friend by your side to encourage you, start by speaking up in situations that require a short response

Summary: Summary (c) is the best summary. It contains only the most important ideas from both paragraphs—feeling some anxiety is normal but feeling a lot of anxiety causes severe physical reactions. Summary (a) does not include the idea of feeling nervous. Summary (b) does not include the idea of feeling anxiety. Both (a) and (b) include examples.

Vocabulary: 1. d **2.** b **3.** c

Mini-Lesson: (p. 56) 1a. 18 **1b.** 10 **1c.** 10 **Conclusion:** a **2a.** 18 **2b.** 13 **2c.** 10 **Conclusion:** b **3a.** 20 **3b.** 18 **3c.** 7 **Conclusion:** b

Literacy Practice: (p. 47) 1. T **2.** T **3.** F **4.** F **5.** T

Dictionary: 1. T **2.** F **3.** T **4.** F **5.** F

Environment

Unit 7. Tree Planting

Discussion: 1. Student responses will vary. **2a.** Soil improved so people could grow more crops. More trees meant more firewood for cooking and heating. Water was cleaner. The environment was healthier. **2b**. Women earned some money. They were empowered to make changes in their communities. They had a voice and a way to force political change. **3a.** A lack of good soil, trees, and clean water means people cannot grow or cook enough food. They cook with contaminated water. They become hungry and sick. **3b.** They cannot work or support their families because of poor health, so they become poorer.

4. A hummingbird is too small to put out a forest fire, but it can put out a bit of the fire by trying and not giving up. Wangari was one woman who made a lot of changes by not giving up. **5.** Student responses will vary.

Summary: Summary (c) is the best summary. It contains the most important ideas from both paragraphs—the Green Belt movement, the empowerment of women, and women forced political change. Summary (a) does not include the idea of women and empowerment. It contains an example showing one way the government was corrupt. Summary (b) includes the idea of empowerment and women but also includes a quote.

Vocabulary: 1. b **2.** b **3.** d

Mini-Lesson: (p. 66) Solution: Wangari formed the Green Belt Movement or women planted millions of trees. **Results:** Planting trees improved the environment (reduced soil erosion, restored woodlands, cleaned up the waterways) and empowered women (to be keepers of the environment and to stand up for their rights). **(p. 67) Solution:** Wangari fought the government (led protest marches, blockaded forests). **Results**: Protesters were beaten, jailed, and threatened, but they forced political change.

Literacy Practice: 1. Volunteer Rates and Organizations **2a.** 20,000 **2b.** If more people are involved in the study, you can put more trust in the results because you have more data. **3**. 10 **4.** percentage of volunteers in each organization **5**. The dark bar represents immigrant volunteers; the light bar represents Canadian-born volunteers **6.** Knowing who collected the data (the source of information) helps you decide how reliable or true the information is. **7a.** ii **7b.** Possible responses: People born in Canada know how and where to find volunteer work. They have more time to spend on volunteering. Newer immigrants might not speak English well so are not confident enough to volunteer. Immigrants may come from a country where the idea of volunteering is not common. **8a.** i **8b.** Possible responses: Immigrants are a minority, so they need to be politically active to make sure their voice is heard. Immigrants may have come from a country that is oppressed, so once in Canada, they take advantage of being able to be active in politics. **9a.** and **9b.** Student responses will vary. **10.** environment **11a.** The environment is not a priority in terms of choosing volunteer work. **11b.** Possible responses: There are limited environmental organizations to volunteer with. Environmental organizations do not have a lot of money to promote their cause and recruit volunteers. People tend to volunteer more in organizations that are related more directly to their daily lives.

Dictionary: 1. F **2.** T **3.** T **4.** F **5.** F

Unit 8. Community Gardens

Discussion: 1. Student responses will vary. **2.** Food is shipped great distances and transport costs are high. Food deliveries are not reliable because of the weather, which leads to food shortages and higher prices. **3.** The greenhouse provides an opportunity to garden in a place where outdoor gardening is difficult. People can grow a wider variety of fresh produce at cheaper prices. Plants and flowers from the greenhouse beautify the town. The greenhouse is a community centre that brings people together. **4.** Possible response: The second floor is used to grow plants and flowers. Selling these plants and flowers provides the community with a way to support the greenhouse. **5. Steps to start a community garden:** Possible responses: find out how many people are interested in starting a garden, find a location, have a meeting to promote why the garden is a good idea, visit other community gardens for ideas and information, find out about costs and how to get supplies, find out about legal procedures

Vocabulary: 1. a 2. b 3. d

Mini-Lesson: (p. 76) Results for Solution 1: Vegetables were still missing. The gardeners had to remove the broken gate, which was too expensive to repair. **Solution 2:** The gardeners set aside a public lot (and invited people to harvest vegetables from it). **Results for Solution 2:** No vegetables were missing from the gardeners' plots. A thank-you sign appeared. **(p. 77) Results for Solution 1:** Food travels long distances, so it is expensive. Food deliveries are sporadic, so stores do not always have fresh produce. **Solution 2:** The community built a greenhouse. **Results for Solution 2:** People can grow and harvest a variety of fresh produce at affordable prices. (The greenhouse has also become a community centre. Plants and flowers from the greenhouse make the town beautiful.)

Literacy Practice: 1. 8 **2a.** 2 **2b.** 4 **2c.** $3.96 (+ tax) **2d.** 4 **2e.** 2 **2f.** $4.90 (+ tax) **3.** No. Most people already have salt and pepper, so they do not have to buy it just for the recipe. The amount of salt and pepper needed is very small, so it would not make a big difference in the cost of the soup. **4.** Possible responses: Making soup takes a long time. Sometimes you have to buy a spice (e.g. Italian seasoning) that you do not use a lot, which could be expensive. **5.** Possible responses: Yes. Frozen corn is healthier because it has less salt than canned corn. No. Frozen corn is more expensive than canned corn. **6.** No. Fresh vegetables are often more expensive in the winter. The price of vegetables also varies depending on whether the vegetables are imported, local, or organically grown. **7.** Student responses will vary.

Dictionary: 1. F 2. T 3. F 4. T 5. T

History

Unit 9. The Japanese Canadians in World War II

Discussion: 1. Student responses will vary. **2.** The bombing of Pearl Harbor gave racist members of the BC government an excuse to remove Japanese Canadians from the BC coast. The government reacted to the fear and panic of many Canadians. **3. Before:** The BC government passed many laws that made life hard. (Japanese Canadians could not vote. They were barred from most professions. They were paid less than their white co-workers.) **During:** Japanese Canadians lost their jobs. (The Navy, the Canadian Pacific Railway, and other industries fired Japanese Canadian workers.) Schools and newspapers were shut down. Japanese Canadian families were relocated. Many families were separated. (Japanese Canadians had to live in relocation camps. Some lived as prisoners in internment camps. Men worked on sugar beet farms and in road-building camps.) **After:** The BC government made Japanese Canadians leave the province. The government deported 4,000 Japanese Canadians. **4.** Possible responses: There was not enough public pressure to force the government to apologize. What happened to the Japanese Canadians was forgotten by the public or believed to be unimportant. By apologizing, the government would be admitting to racism. After 45 years, it was easier to apologize because the government that finally apologized did not feel directly responsible. **5.** Student responses will vary.

Summary: Summary (b) is the best summary. It contains the important ideas from both paragraphs—Japanese immigrants hoped for a better life in Canada and the BC government passed racist laws. Summary (a) does not include the key idea of racism. Summary (c) includes the important ideas, but it also includes an example of a racist law.

Vocabulary: 1. a **2.** d **3.** c

Mini-Lesson: 1. 1930 **2.** 1990 **3.** 2000 **4.** 60 **5.** about 6 years **6.** b **7a.** No. The government started to deport Japanese Canadians after the war ended. Japanese Canadians were not free to live where they wanted until 1949. **7b.** Student responses will vary. **8a.** about 43 **8b.** Student responses will vary.

Literacy Practice: Student responses will vary.

Dictionary: 1. T **2.** T **3.** F **4.** F **5.** F

10. Residential Schools

Discussion: 1. Student responses will vary. **2.** Compulsory attendance meant the students were away from the culture of their communities for long periods of time. Students could not practise their traditions or speak their language. The schools taught white customs, languages (English and French), and religion (Christianity). **3. Children:** suffered different kinds of abuse; lost their culture; felt ashamed of their culture; could not fit into their communities or cope in white society; turned to addictions; learned basic skills in reading and writing; learned housework, trades, and how to farm **Families:** were separated; former students had trouble raising their own children **4.** Possible responses: Students were torn from their families so they had no parenting role models to follow. The nuns in residential schools did not model love, caring, or compassion. **5.** Student responses will vary.

Summary: Summary (c) is the best summary. It contains the most important idea from the paragraph—Aboriginal students suffered abuse and these abuses had negative effects on their lives. Summaries (a) and (b) do not include the idea of abuse. They only include an example of how Aboriginal students were affected by the residential schools.

Vocabulary: 1. d **2.** a **3.** c

Mini-Lesson: (p. 96) Paragraph time markers: in September 1944; Six years later; for the next 10 years; By the early 1970s; In 1997; Ten years later; In the same year **1.** 16 **2.** about 27 years old **3.** 2007 **(p. 97) Events on timeline:** late 1800s (government passes laws to assimilate Indians); 1876 (government passes Indian Act); 1931 (80 residential schools are in operation); 1990 (Fontaine lobbies for compensation); 1996 (last school closes); 2007 (courts agree to a compensation package); 2008 (government apologizes)

Literacy Practice: 1. Janet Dick, a First Nations woman who attended a residential school **2.** She feels that she has been silenced all her life. She wants a voice, which is the poem. **3.** the writer, the residential school nuns (or authorities), people (family, elders) from the writer's community **4.** Possible answers: The writer is asking for a voice because she has been silenced for so long. The school nuns are saying, "Quiet! Hush! Don't speak!" because they are in control and forbid the writer to voice thoughts or speak in her language. The people from the writer's community tell the writer to be still, quiet (not ask questions) and to learn the white culture. They do not want the writer to shame them by speaking out. **5.** Students responses will vary. **6.** Student responses will vary.

Dictionary: 1. F **2.** T **3.** F **4.** T **5.** T